Vehicular Ad Hoc Networks (VANETs) in Intelligent Transportation Systems

rodger kimberley

CHAPTER 1

INTRODUCTION

1.1 VEHICULAR AD HOC NETWORKS – AN INTRODUCTION

Traffic safety is a crucial priority for several nations. The new traffic laws and better infrastructure have been implemented in the countries; however, there are pathetic improvements in traffic safety. In turn, the most effective approach is the introduction of modern technologies to prevent accidents. The current developments in wireless technology and the car industry have triggered the rise of the Vehicular Ad Hoc Networks (VANETs) as a key area of research. The key goal of VANETs is the enhancement of traffic safety. Currently, some VANET applications have been envisaged to extend vehicular capabilities and improve the driving experience as a way of implementing Intelligent Transportation Systems (ITS) [1].

Due to the inherent interest of mobile computing technologies, VANET is a major wireless networking paradigm of vehicular communication. VANET is an intelligent component of the transportation system that is equipped with communication equipment known as On-Board Units (OBUs) and Road-side Units (RSUs). RSUs are positioned on the side of the road, and they serve as an entry point to the network. Due to its immense potential to enhance the efficiency of traffic and automobile safety by sensing the road conditions and emergency cases, VANET has become a topic of interest to drivers and passengers [2].

VANETs are a subgroup of the Mobile Ad Hoc Networks (MANETs) where the mobile nodes are both stationary and moving automobiles. There are unique features of VANET, such as high velocities of nodes, frequent network fragmentation, and highway-induced constraints, that make VANETs different when compared to traditional MANETs. The unstable movement of the vehicles causes a lack of stability in the inter-vehicle communication links. Information distributed in VANET can be location-based, including fuel stations, traffic jams, rest areas, and toll information, or can be produced by the mobile cars that communicate events of dangerous conditions on the road or other environmental processes.

1.2 VANET ARCHITECTURES

According to IEEE 1471-2000 and ISO/IEC 42010 standards [3], the VANET system architecture consists of three primary components: the mobile field, the infrastructure field, and the generic field (as seen in Figure 1.1).

1. The sphere of mobile technologies is split into two different subdomains: mobile devices and motor vehicles. The vehicle subdomain is considered to be all the vehicular entities, including the automobile, buses, and other transportations. The cell phone subdomain encompasses the use of personal navigation devices, which are very portable, most of which are smartphones.
2. The infrastructure domain includes central technology and roadside technology. Traffic lights form a central part of the road technology industry. The central infrastructure includes infrastructure control centers, vehicle management centers, and traffic management centers.
3. The generic domain combines the use of internet-based resources with the use of the private infrastructure. The VANET has any server, node, or ancillary computational resource subsumed in a generic domain.

Data is sent through mobile networks and processed in the infrastructure sphere using proper modulation. The infrastructure domain then communicates with the generic domain via direct communication links. The methodology allows users to make effective and efficient use of the road infrastructure. The Federal Communications Commission (FCC) has designated the 5.9 GHz frequency for Dedicated Short-Range Communication (DSRC) to provide communication channels between vehicles, stationary RSUs, and OBUs.

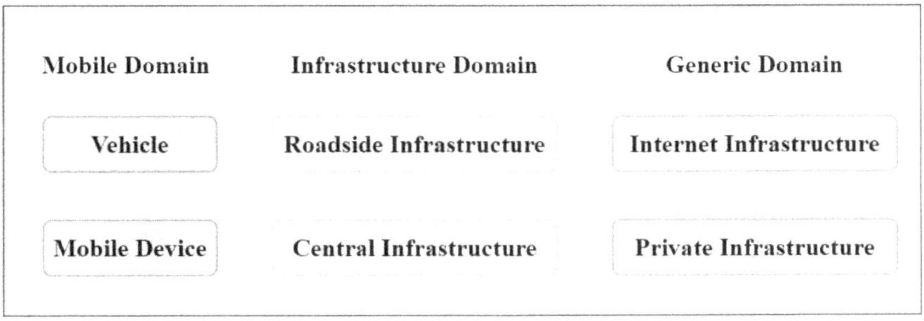

Figure 1.1 VANET Architecture

According to the World Health Organization's (WHO) data on road traffic injuries worldwide, traffic accidents are the leading cause of mortality. By 2030, a safe and secure transportation system shall be developed and provided at a reasonable price for everyone, according to Sustainable Development Goal 11 (SDG-11) [4]. The primary focus is on user groups such as women, children, people with special needs, and the elderly.

To reduce the count of traffic accidents, injuries, and fatalities, a clever and sophisticated traffic management system will be implemented. Through intelligent and smart traffic management systems that send information related to traffic density, traffic congestion, particular route information, accidents, or other information, VANETs will aid in the achievement of SDG-11 [5]. In the VANET communication architecture, vehicles inside the network exchange data using any of the communication architectures listed below.

1. **Vehicle-to-Vehicle (V2V) transmission:** As shown in Figure 1.2, data exchange between cars on the road occurs to exchange and alert drivers to important information for safety-related applications [6].

Figure 1.2 V2V Transmission

2. **Vehicle-to-Infrastructure (V2I) transmission:** Figure 1.3 illustrates the V2I interaction between mobile vehicles and the RSU. It is used to gather environmental and traffic data and communicate it to drivers and passengers [7].

3. **Hybrid transmission:** As shown in Figure 1.4, hybrid transmission entails data sharing between cars, stationary communication devices, and bystanders [8]. In addition to improving driver and passenger safety, hybrid communication in VANET improves network efficiency by delivering data faster.

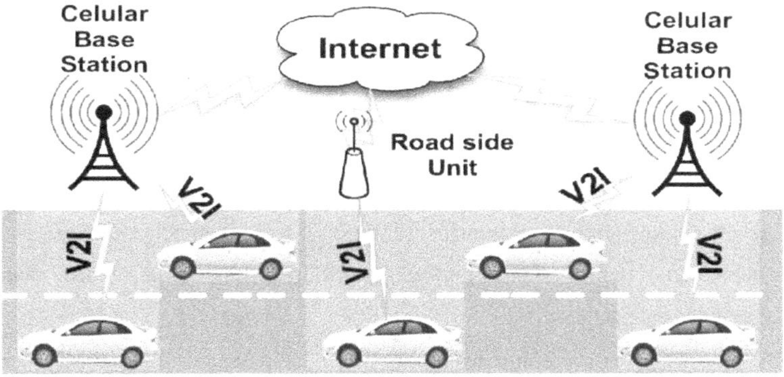

Figure 1.3 V2I Transmission

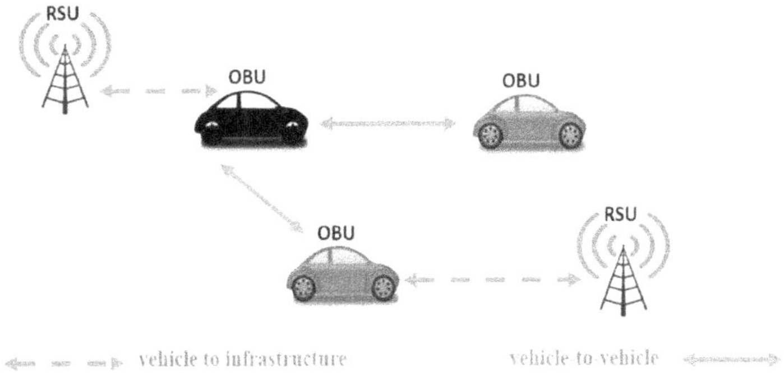

Figure 1.4 Hybrid Transmission

4. **Vehicle-to-Broadband (V2B) transmission:** V2B uses wireless broadband networks, such as 3G, 4G, and 5G, to link cars [9]. Since the cloud has more traffic data and other information, including infotainment and monitoring data, it will be easier for the driver to follow the car.

1.3 VANET TECHNOLOGIES

The DSRC and Wireless Access in Vehicular Environments (WAVE) using the IEEE standard IEEE 802.11p are two wireless technologies developed by several working groups to serve VANET applications. These standards permit the development of specific transportable routing devices by operators in the automobile and telecommunications industries, subject to certain restrictions.

- **DSRC:** It is a widely used wireless standard that was created to facilitate ITS. To transmit messages for safety applications, it connects several VANET topologies [10]. According to DSRC, the FCC set aside a 70 MHz band between 5.850 GHz and 5.925 GHz to deploy wireless systems for V2V and V2I communications. DSRC uses a short-range radio to transmit data at a speed of 27 Mbps, which is much slower than satellite or cellular connections.
- **WAVE:** The primary component of DSRC that illustrates IEEE P1609 standards is WAVE, which focuses on the Medium Access Control (MAC) and network layers to defend against interference from other devices or networks and to assure safety, health, or the environment. WAVE, which is based on IEEE 802.11 standards, is complicated. Radio equipment specified in WAVE to provide or use services includes OBUs (mobile devices) of automobiles and RSUs (stationary devices) at the side of the road [11].
- The 4G Long-Term Evolution (LTE) standard, Bluetooth (IEEE 802.15), and WiMAX (IEEE 802.16) also provide vehicular communication. New protocols such as IPv6 may also be used to prolong these communications [12].

1.4 VANET CHARACTERISTICS

While VANETs retain the features of MANETs, a few unique VANET properties, as presented in Figure 1.5, are outlined and explained below.

1. Highly dynamic nodes: In VANETs, vehicle nodes travel at very high speeds, ranging from 40 km/h to 200 km/h. VANETs are regarded as very dynamic networks because of their highly mobile nodes [13]. The nodes movement is determined by the route's structure and design.
2. Minimal infrastructure requirement: Because VANET is a network made up of vehicle nodes, it is regarded as an infrastructure-less network [14]. Vehicles may communicate with one another without using a physical medium. Because of the

hop-to-hop communication characteristic, the network may be managed without a centralized governing authority.

3. No additional hardware components, such as hubs or switches, are needed. The VANET network requires RSUs and Application Units (AUs) as resources.
4. Self-organized: VANET nodes choose how to send messages on their own. To provide easy information transmission across hops, the node itself handles the switch functions to convey the data [15]. VANETs are self-organized networks because of these features.
5. Dispersed network: RSUs, AUs, and vehicle nodes make up the dispersed network topology of VANETs. Vehicle registration is managed by AUs, which are the top-layer controllers. The VANET network's next tier contains RSUs. Under a single AU, many RSUs are positioned along the edges of the highways [16]. In their respective areas, RSUs are regarded as the regional authority that provides services to the vehicle nodes. The distributed network scenario is made up of all of this structure.
6. Predictable topology: VANETs use the mesh topology to exchange information inside the network since nodes move randomly. It is simple to monitor the runtime, present position, and time of mobile vehicles by utilizing the digital map. It aids in network topology prediction [17].
7. Critical latency: Latency is the amount of time that passes between the transmission of a message from the source node and the reception of the message by the receiver node. High mobility nodes in different directions may only remain in the association for a brief amount of time in VANETs. The primary requirement is that the message reach the target vehicle node within the allotted time. Therefore, low-latency characteristics must be included in the VANET network architecture [18].
8. Road safety and traffic efficiency: As the number of cars continues to rise, it becomes more difficult to systematically manage traffic. Road safety and traffic efficiency are achieved via VANETs' direct communications capabilities and minimal infrastructure requirements [19].
9. Traveler comfort: The VANET network easily supplies information about traffic flow, traffic congestion, regions with high or low traffic, accident alerts, information about the closest retail centers, food intersections, music playback, and more. The traveler is comfortable thanks to all of these characteristics.

10. Network density: The random movement of vehicles causes variations in network density. For light traffic, the network density is low; for heavy traffic, it is high.

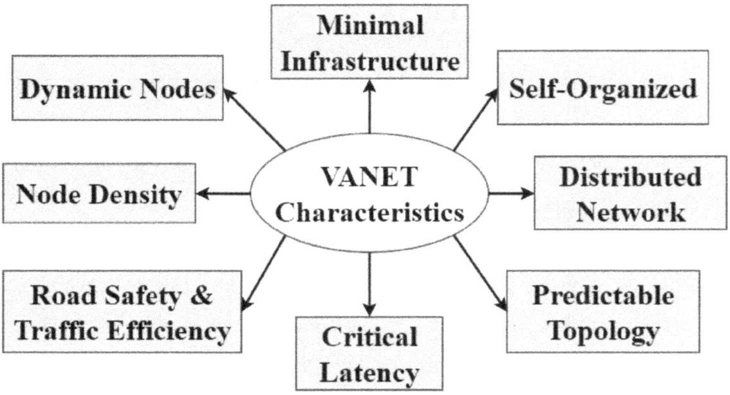

Figure 1.5 VANET Characteristics

1.5 VANET APPLICATIONS

Numerous applications associated with the traffic data, driver convenience, vehicle supervision, etc., are supported by VANETs. Additionally, VANETs have a few infotainments uses. The next generation of intelligent and smart transportation is triggered by a variety of VANET applications, which also significantly improve the transportation system [20]. The construction of intelligent transportation systems often employs VANETs due to their practical uses. Applications for VANETs have made them very popular, much like those of Wireless Sensor Networks (WSNs).

Several VANET applications, including traffic safety, traffic efficiency, traffic enhancement, etc., were shown by Pandey et al. [21]. Transportation safety provides a variety of alarm messages in an emergency. Lane change assistance, collision warnings, overtaking warnings, and other alerts are examples of these. By monitoring and evaluating changing traffic conditions, traffic efficiency aims to support and enhance traffic flow. By sharing traffic information among cars, cooperative driving and accident avoidance are two examples of traffic improvement. These applications are crucial in preventing the many fatalities that may result from traffic accidents daily. Apart from these uses, VANETs are also often used for location-based services, toll services, and entertainment applications. As a result, both public and private organizations have begun making financial investments in this field.

To improve safety and transportation systems and provide drivers and passengers in cars with more comfort, these organizations have launched a number of initiatives. These days, new-generation communication technologies installed in cars greatly enhance vehicle-to-vehicle connection. Healthcare, military communication, pandemic control, and other fields utilize VANETs due to their enhanced capabilities. Researchers are increasingly favoring VANETs due to their diverse applications. Enhancing vehicle communication has consistently piqued the attention of academia and industry.

1.5.1 Transportation Safety

The need for transportation safety, which relies on high-rate safety messaging or beaconing, primarily motivates the development of vehicle communication systems. Reducing the likelihood of accidents and fatalities is the primary goal of every transportation safety application. Vehicles and RSUs may share information on how to do this. Lane change assistance, overtaking vehicle warning, head-on collision warning, rear-end collision warning, cooperative collision warning exchange, emergency vehicle alert, pre-crash sensing, wrong-way driving warning, traffic condition warning, etc. are examples of common transportation safety features [22]. Sending emergency alerts to the contact center, which then relays the information to other responding bodies, is another way to ensure safety. Occasionally, live video transmission via car cameras, etc., may be necessary for emergency services to respond more effectively. Figure 1.6 displays the following list of safety application types.

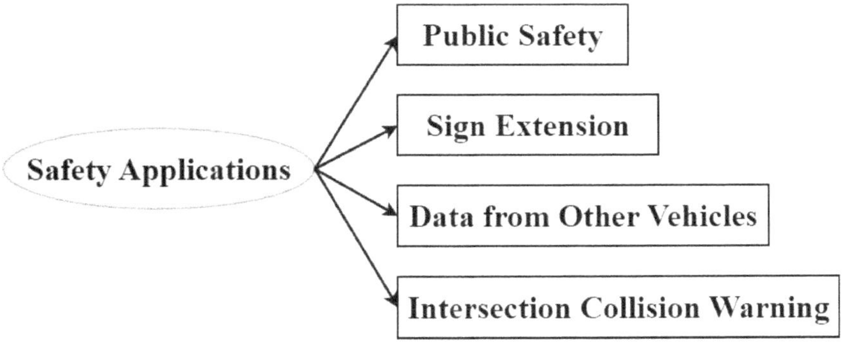

Figure 1.6 Safety Applications

- **Public safety:** The team in charge of emergency response is the public safety application. The best route information also helps in reducing the time taken by the driver during an emergency, like accidents, ambulance calls, fire department calls, police calls, and other related emergencies [23]. The frequency of public safety applications is 5.9 GHz, and the communication range is 300-1000 m. The RSU and the OBU of other cars nearby send emergency warning signals to the driver about any form of emergency service; hence, the vehicle can arrive at the desired destination without unnecessary delays. The information to be transmitted includes the vehicle speed, route, heading, and other relevant information, and it is transmitted by RSUs within the network.

a. Emergency vehicle signal pre-emption: The traffic structure of virtual ad hoc vehicle networks has been carefully structured in such a way that it minimizes the chances of casualties in the case of ambulance vehicles. RSUs also relay messages to turn the traffic lights green in cases where emergency vehicles are on the way to a red signal, thus permitting faster movement of emergency vehicles [24].
b. Post-crash alert: When a collision or other incident on the roadway occurs, the impacted vehicle exchanges with nearby RSUs or the other vehicles on the roadway to send out a warning. This warning enables the other vehicles to reroute or expect an extra travel duration, and V2V and V2I interactions transmit the message across the network [25].

- **Sign extension:** Through the use of roadside signs, sign extension, and a safety application of VANETs, warns users and drivers to prevent collisions [26]. Sign extension uses a frequency band of 5.9 GHz to support the transmission of messages on the wavelength range of 100 to 500 m. There are many uses for this sign extension, as listed below:

a. The RSUs are particularly important in transmitting the message to car occupants within the area, notifying them about low parking zones. In the case where a vehicle tries to enter a low-parking area, an RSU sends a warning message about the unavailability of a parking space that is then received by the driver, hence guaranteeing situational awareness and adherence to parking rules.
b. RSUs in the field of emergency braking transmit hazard information to the drivers facing unfavorable weather conditions like smoke, fog, or rain. This safety application reduces sudden, rough deceleration, like a major cause of traffic accidents, by making possible a controlled, gradual braking reaction,

which will lead to a statistically significant decrease in the number of accidents.

c. The in-vehicle AMBER alert system is a vital safety mechanism, as it will alert the drivers to the existence of suspicious or potentially dangerous vehicles in the network. This kind of real-time surveillance will augment guards against threats by unknown parties on the road. An AMBER alert message is sent to all cars within range of the suspicious vehicle and to all vehicles on the same route whenever law enforcement officials see a suspicious vehicle (one that has been engaged in or registered for a crime). The other drivers on that road are better protected by this practice [27].

d. Low-bridge warning: RSUs positioned close to the bridges send low-bridge warning information. Vehicles obtain alert signals from RSUs that provide details on the bridge's height, length, commencement, and departure. It facilitates the driver's decision to either follow the bridge path or alter their route to avoid it.

- **Data from other vehicles and RSUs:** Using a frequency of 5.9 GHz, the safety application of data from other cars and RSUs functions in a frequency range of 50 to 100 m. The effect of this phenomenon is that it is an easy way of facilitating the smooth running of traffic, increasing a quantifiable level of traffic safety, and delivering ancillary information on traffic assistance. The information obtained about other cars may include:

a. Cooperative forward collision warning: This warning system uses V2V communication to send the warning message to cars that are in the accident orbit, which keeps the accident from happening. Cautionary warnings indicate the exact location of the accident, other ways to arrive there, how long it will take to reconstruct the route, and other useful information [28]. The goal of all these things is to make traffic move more smoothly.

b. Car sensors set up runtime data for detecting before a crash. OBUs and RSUs use computing processes to predict the precise position of the accident site based on this data. OBUs and RSUs notify the cars traveling that particular route in advance of any road condition warning messages. When traveling in rural regions, where roads are often uneven, this app is a huge help.

c. Intersection collision avoidance: VANETs lower the incidence of traffic collisions by predicting the collision chance analytically. The intersection collision avoidance application uses a frequency of 5.9 GHz and works in a bandwidth of 200 to 300 m.

- **Intersection collision warning:** RSUs gather data on junction locations and road mesh. By using calculations on the sensor data and information about road junction positions, intersection collision alerts are forecasted [29].
    a. The system prevents stop sign violations by alerting cars approaching the stop signs. The information gathered by surrounding cars and RSUs is used to calculate the run duration of the distance between the stoplights and vehicles. The corresponding cars receive warning messages based on the computations. It reduces the number of stop signal violations.
    b. Data on pedestrian crossings: The sensors mounted on RSUs determine where the pedestrian crossing is located on the street [30]. The extracted information informs vehicles within that range or those approaching within it. It helps regulate vehicle speed appropriately to prevent collisions.

1.5.2 Traffic Efficiency and Management

By offering traffic assistance, these apps concentrate on enhancing the flow of traffic on the roads. Traffic management apps keep an eye on the driver to regulate the vehicle's speed for comfortable driving and to prevent needless braking. By tracking and sharing vehicle navigation, cooperative navigation helps improve traffic efficiency [31]. A motorist must take emergency notifications and traffic into account while driving to increase traffic efficiency. Traffic management handles other scenarios, such as junctions and crossroads. Vehicles must communicate at crosspoints and road crossings to prevent unplanned accidents. This aids the driver in increasing driving efficiency. In addition to all of these uses, one area where VANETs are crucial and improve traffic efficiency is road congestion management. Using the current traffic conditions, road congestion management determines the optimal route dynamically toward the goal.

1.5.3 Comfort Driving

To make driving easier, it contains data that may be shared between cars or between vehicles and stationary nodes. Via vehicular communication, a small number of pertinent details are sent to cars, such as weather reports, locations of gas stations, parking lots, dining establishments, road charging stations, route guidance, etc. Additionally, several commercials and announcements may be shown to all or a select group of cars. Figure 1.7 displays a few VANET comfort applications.

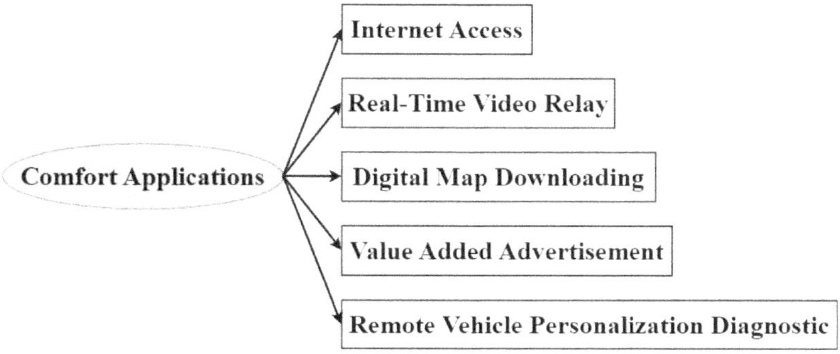

Figure 1.7 Comfort Applications

- Internet access: RSU serves as a router in VANETs. In a dispersed network, RSUs provide an effective internet service. For V2I and V2V communication, every vehicle in the network uses the internet.
- Remote car personalization diagnostics: The user may operate in customized car settings thanks to comfort apps. Users may submit diagnostic data from automobiles to AUs over the internet [32].
- Downloading digital maps: RSUs facilitate the use of digital maps by both drivers and passengers in moving and stationary vehicles. Digital maps of the region are available for download and use as needed.
- VANET comfort apps provide real-time video relays. Users (passengers or drivers) can use the on-demand real-time video relay capability to amuse themselves while waiting or relaxing during their trip. This application is hosted jointly by AU and RSU [33].
- Value-added advertising: The value-added advertising function makes the user experience more comfortable. Passengers benefit from being aware of the ads displayed by nearby retail establishments, gas stations, hospitals, dining areas, etc. In value-added advertising, RSUs are essential [34].

1.5.4 Infotainment Applications

The goal of interactive entertainment is to share information about entertainment with other drivers and passengers. Infotainment applications might be either internet-based or local. Typical examples of local services include local media downloads, point-of-interest alerts, and local e-commerce. Fleet management, parking zone management, insurance management, and other financial services are among the internet-based services. Infotainment apps may also include several other applications in a distributed environment, such as file-sharing, chat, and distributed gaming [35].

1.5.5 Urban Sensing

Monitoring traffic in urban areas and exchanging data based on shared interests are examples of urban sensing. According to Cuff et al. [36], all cars are outfitted with onboard sensors and additional Global Positioning System (GPS) devices as part of a vehicular network utilized for urban sensing. A vehicle network, which is crucial to urban sensing, is used to record the environmental conditions and many social activities that take place in urban environments. When smart devices are combined with OBUs that are deployed with automobiles in VANETs, urban sensing becomes crucial. Virtual sensor networks pose different challenges compared to conventional wireless sensor networks. Thus, if cars are outfitted with powerful processing units, various communication devices, navigation systems, other sensor devices, etc., this seems to be a lucrative study subject in the near future. VANETs have enormous potential for widespread use when sensor networks and vehicle networks are combined.

1.6 ISSUES IN VANET

VANET introduces several difficulties, including MAC, data administration, storage, mobility, data aggregation, validation, Quality of Service (QoS) delivery, routing, security, and privacy [37, 38].

1. MAC: In VANET, sharing the transmission medium efficiently is a complicated challenge to prevent accidents due to rapid vehicle movement and network changes. Cognitive radio technology and Time Division Multiple Access (TDMA)-based MAC techniques minimize interference from concurrent transmission. Different MAC protocols in VANET may be used to reduce collisions caused by transmission, as well as hidden and exposed terminal difficulties.

2. Vehicle movement in VANET is more uncertain than in MANET. Frequent connections and disconnections occur in a matter of seconds. So, exchanging information in a short period of time is a significant barrier. Sophisticated mobility models for vehicle interaction are necessary.
3. Data management and storage: VANET, which includes automobiles and other devices, creates a considerable volume of data due to the increased number of nodes. As a result, researchers working on VANET have additional challenges in data storage and administration. Data management and big data analysis are among the solutions available to address this problem.
4. Data aggregation combines information from several nodes before reallocating them. The limited bandwidth in the VANET scenario necessitates information aggregation for efficient data processing and dissemination without network overhead. Clustering of nodes is one proposed solution to the data aggregation issue in VANETs.
5. Validation of data: VANET's diverse vehicle population reduces the risk of malicious traffic and improves network performance. Hence, validation of data is a primary priority in VANET.
6. QoS delivery: VANET's dynamic nature causes large variations in node location, distance, and connection. Thus, designing and developing methods to improve service quality in VANET is a significant challenge.
7. Routing: In VANET, routing is the process of selecting the most efficient path for a message to reach its destination. Routing protocols are intended to facilitate communication between VANET nodes. If the vehicles are not in the same communication range, different routing techniques are used to effectively transport data packets to their destinations. The primary goal of an effective routing algorithm is to eliminate End-to-End (E2E) delays and network management overheads caused by rapid vehicle movement, frequent link disconnection, and blockages.
8. Security and privacy: Vehicle sensors retain personal information and track position, ensuring data privacy. Hackers may exploit the information and modify it. As a result, security and privacy are major challenges for safety applications.

1.7 ROUTING IN VANET

Routing is defined as the choosing of an appropriate route for delivering data packets to their destination successfully. Much research is being conducted to optimize VANET routing while taking into account the numerous factors and problematic elements of VANETs. Because of frequent network modifications and variations in vehicle density, many routing techniques have been created [39].

Routing messages from one vehicle to another is one of the most serious issues in VANETs. Traditional routing and transmission techniques are intended for fully linked networks. Although VANETs are a subtype of MANETs, they exhibit distinct features owing to their high mobility and defined routes. As a result, protocols designed for fixed networks and MANETs are ineffective and inefficient in VANETs.

VANET routing protocols are anticipated to enable large-scale automotive traffic, high vehicle mobility, and frequent connection failures.

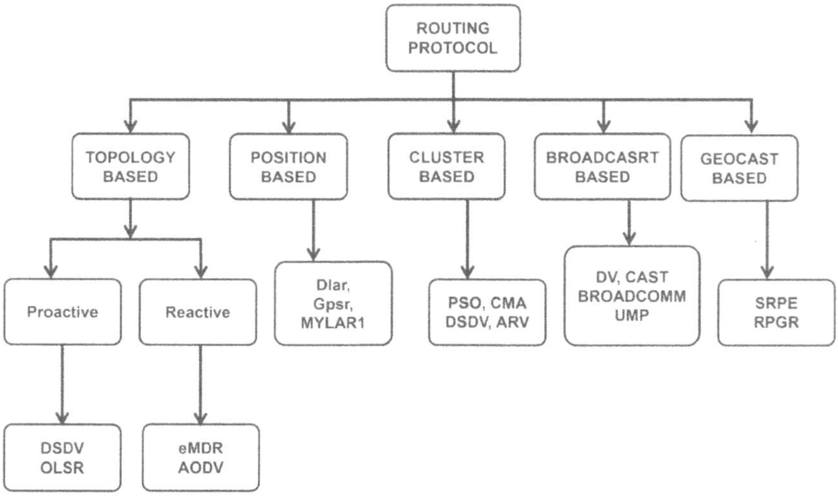

Figure 1.8 Taxonomy of VANETs Routing Protocols

Several routing protocols have previously been developed to enable effective and dependable routing between cars. Figure 1.8 depicts multiple criteria-based classifications of routing protocols.

Routing protocols may be divided into three categories depending on the distinct network architectures of VANETs: hierarchical routing, flat routing, and positional routing. According to [40], these protocols may be further divided into two types depending on the routing methodologies used: proactive and reactive routing protocols. Protocols are divided into three types: unicast, multicast, and broadcast routing protocols.

Similarly, routing protocols may be divided into two types depending on the routing information employed in packet forwarding: geographically based and topology-based routing protocols. Furthermore, classifications can be made based on service quality, and routing protocols can be divided into three categories: handling different network topologies (flat, hierarchical, and geographical), dealing with different route discovery mechanisms (proactive, reactive, hybrid, and predictive), and finally dealing with MAC layer communication [41].

1.8 TAXONOMY OF ROUTING PROTOCOLS IN VANET

All routing protocols may be divided into groups based on several factors. The routing protocols for VANETs are generally divided into four categories: position-based, topology-based, cluster-based, multicast/geographic-based, and multipath, and broadcast-based routing. These are described below sections.

1.8.1 Position-Based Routing Protocols

Position-based routing methods rely on the geographical location of cars, which is determined by street maps and other navigation aids. This kind of routing method is also known as geographical routing. Vehicle location data is critical for determining the best path from source to destination. When generating routes, these methods leverage the real location of cars in VANETs to determine the next hop [42]. It does not have a routing table to keep routing information current.

These protocols ascertain the position or location of the cars using a variety of sources, including maps and GPS. Consequently, the source and destination rely on the status of the nodes to send and receive messages. Information discovery, route preservation, and topology maintenance are not necessary for this class of protocols. Consequently, the two primary components of transmitted packets are location and packet forwarding. Greedy Perimeter Stateless Routing (GPSR) and Reliability Improving Position-based Routing (RIPR) are two common examples of this family of protocols.

- GPSR: Wireless and mobile networks benefit greatly from the GPSR routing technology. This approach considers geographic routing factors [43, 44]. GPSR employs two techniques for data forwarding: greedy forwarding and perimeter forwarding. When greedy forwarding is not possible because there are no nearby nodes except the current one (see Figure 1.9b), the second method is used. By default, the first procedure (see Figure 1.9a) sends the packet to the destination's closest neighbor node. The perimeter mode allows GPSR to apply the right-hand rule to move packets around holes without a nearest neighbor. This protocol makes judgments based on the hop-by-hop principle rather than requiring the creation of a comprehensive point-to-point link.

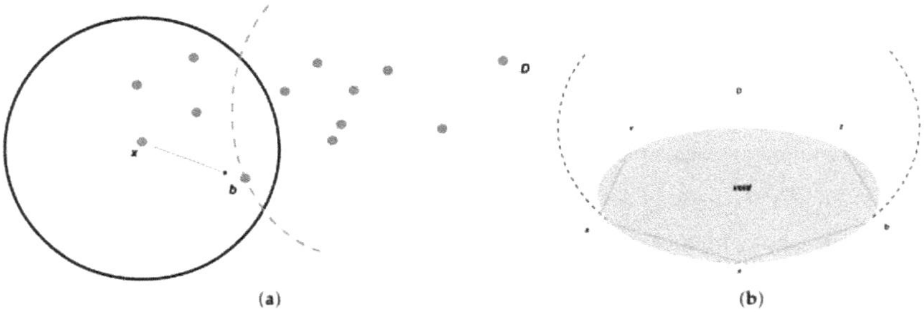

Figure 1.9 GPSR Functions: (a) Scenario of Greedy Forwarding and (b) Node x is Void related to Destination D in Perimeter Mode

- RIPR: It was developed to provide a solution for several link failures [45]. This protocol determines the direction and speed of a vehicle's motion. The next neighbor cluster's location and speed are then noted in a routing table that is kept at each node. Until it reaches the destination, the source node selects the closest neighbor based on the items in its table. The decision-making of the intermediate nodes, which make further hops, is improved by the strategy employed to determine the next hop node. In this protocol, the speed of vehicular mobility is also taken into account.

1.8.2 Topology-Based Routing Protocols

Topology-based routing algorithms rank among the notable routing algorithms in ad hoc networks. These standards take advantage of the global network architecture knowledge and still maintain the link-level information. In these algorithms, every node within a VANET has a routing table which contains information on paths to all possible destinations. Topology based techniques can additionally be divided into proactive, reactive and hybrid methods all of which have a number of different routing techniques. The mentioned method of routing mainly covers the latest developments.

- Proactive routing protocols: Every node in this protocol has a routing table where the routing data is stored. The mobility of nodes is very high, which makes it critical whenever nodes enter or exit the network and links are broken and later restored. In proactive protocols, routing tables are maintained up to date and reachable by use of update steps, but this overhead may negatively impact network throughput [46]. They are Destination Sequence Distance Vector (DSDV), Optimized Link State Routing (OLSR) and Fiskeye State Routing (FSR).
  - DSDV: DSDV is based on Bellman-Ford algorithm. This technique supports a complete table of paths to all the known destinations using collaborative participation of every node [47, 48]. Quick adverts are that which are used to notify neighbors of topological changes. The DSDV updates the database progressively when just deltas are transmitted to other nodes by a node, or entirely when all information is transmitted by a node to other nodes. Working of DSDV protocol is shown in Figure 1.10.

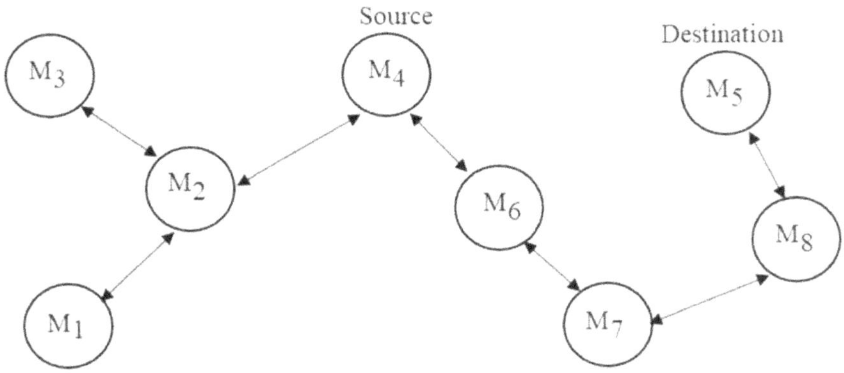

Figure 1.10 DSDV Routing Protocol

- OLSR: This protocol requires every node to maintain a list of neighbors that it occasionally accesses through one or two hops [49]. To minimize the number of active relays required to reach every 2-hop neighbor, a Multi-Point Relay (MPR) is utilized. Consequently, a node transmits a packet if it is selected as a relay point via the source node. For this, the MPR algorithm was employed. The link state packets are exchanged to generate the routing tables and maintain them in OLSR once the selected relay nodes are put into place. Consequently, active routes to any point in the network are reached once the algorithm has stabilized. Figure 1.11 shows the working of OLSR protocol.

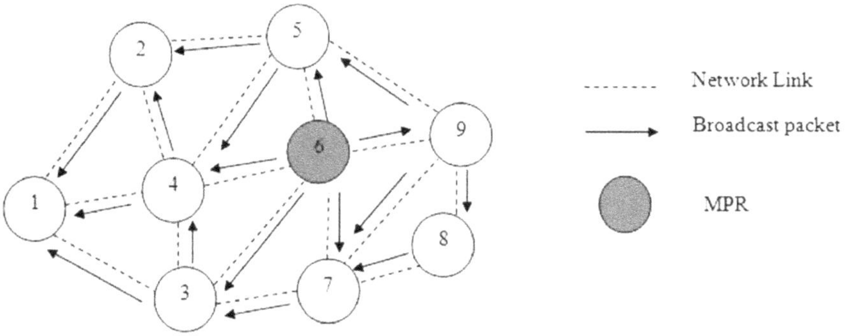

Figure 1.11 Working of OLSR Protocol

- Reactive routing protocols: These protocols simply assist in route discovery when sending data packets from an origin node to a destination node; they do not create a new routing database. When a message needs to be sent to a certain location, flooding is used to start the route-finding process. An answer message is returned to the origin after the communication has arrived at its destination. These protocols result in reduced control message overflow, but they also slow down the route-finding process. Ad-hoc On-Demand Distance Vector (AODV) routing and AODV+Preferred Group Broadcast (PGB) routing is an illustration of a reactive protocol.
  - AODV: This protocol was developed mainly for mobile ad hoc networks, or MANETs. This protocol is reactive since it only creates channels in response to anode requests to transfer packets [50, 51]. Figure 1.12 illustrates a common procedure methodology. To collect

current routing information, it uses sequence numbers, standard routing tables, and an entry for each destination. AODV saves the routes once the nodes (source-destination) establish a connection, despite the source's desire to send data. The primary route discovery phase of this protocol involves sending Route Request (RREQ) packets from the input node to other nodes to determine the destination node. The RREQ source receives Route Reply (RREP) packets in unicast mode. The absolute path is created to save information in the middle molecules with the route in. The absolute path is created to preserve data in the middle way nodes with the route in the local routing table. A communication failure can also be reported via Route Error (RERR) messages. This is where a new cycle of route-finding has to begin. To ascertain and monitor connectivity with neighboring nodes, Hello messages should always be used.

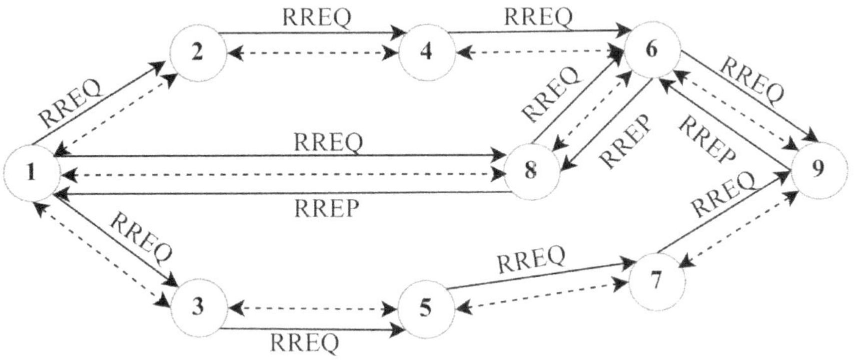

Figure 1.12 Typical Working of AODV Routing Protocol

- AODV+PGB: To cut down on communication overhead, it makes use of PGB [52]. It provides more persistent routing than AODV. PGB receivers can ascertain whether they belong to an ideal group and which node in the set wishes to communicate because this protocol is made to lessen the high communication cost brought on by the AODV route discovery cycle. The communication signal identifies the node.

- Hybrid routing protocols: Hybrid routing, as its name suggests, combines proactive and reactive routing techniques [53]. This category of protocols aims to reduce the time it takes to determine a path between two locations. Protocols such as the Zone Routing Protocol (ZRP) and the Zone-based Hierarchical Link State (ZHLS) routing protocol fall under this category.
  - **ZRP:** When communication between nearby nodes is necessary, ZRP employs both the active and reactive routing strategies in the area of the anode. Intra-Zone Routing Protocol (IARP) establishes contact with nearby neighborhoods [54]. In another situation, the IERP is utilized to establish communication across zones. Consequently, proactive routing is utilized to provide routes inside a region or neighborhood, whereas reactive routing looks for routes based on demand when it's important to provide communications to other locations.
  - **ZHLS:** Another routing protocol in this set of protocols is ZHLS [55]. ZHLS divides the network into non-overlapping zones based on node position information. In this protocol, each node knows its neighbors and the connectivity of its network region. Information about the nodes and the zones' connectivity is disseminated across the network. As a result, the node and zone IDs can be used to create the route.

1.8.3 Cluster-Based Routing Protocols

Cluster-based routing in VANETs improves network scalability by effectively separating a single big network into numerous sub-networks depending on certain criteria [56]. Sub-networks (also called clusters) consist of those vehicles that have common characteristics like direction and speed. The Cluster Head (CH) enables communication between clusters by coordinating with other nodes in the VANET.

The mentioned protocols try to divide network nodes into distinct clusters. As a result, a cluster consists of closely spaced nodes, with one vehicle serving as the cluster's leader. The processes used to construct a cluster determine its extent. In other words, the network can be clustered by the number of cars, their proximity, and their speed and direction. After segmentation, cluster nodes select the CH, who is responsible for overseeing the cluster and facilitating inter-cluster communication. As a result, during inter-cluster communication, communications are routed to the most appropriate nearby cluster.

- Location-cluster-based flooding routing algorithm: The network's nodes are divided into clusters by this protocol [57]. Communication between each cluster and its fellow cluster chiefs will thereafter be arranged by the CH. To update their parameters, the CHs also periodically send beacon signals. CHs also send out location request packets to gather location information for other clusters. Pointing out that this routing architecture, which was designed to enable V2V communication, is reactive.

1.8.4 Multipath Routing Protocols

A multipath strategy maintains many routes between the source and destination vehicles. Multipath routing has many benefits, including greater throughput, improved bandwidth usage, and lower congestion [58]. These features make multipath routing more efficient and dependable. Multipath routing schemes are very effective for load balancing in VANETs since they transfer data over numerous pathways concurrently.

1.8.5 Multicast/Geographic Routing Protocols

The forwarding or transmission of data in a location that is appropriate for or relevant to the data that has to be transmitted is the foundation of this family of routing protocols [59]. Position-based multicast is used to send the packets to the cars in the Zone of Relevance (ZOR), which is where the vehicles get the geocast message. To put it another way, the Geo-cast routing protocol distributes data packets from a single source node to all nodes within the appropriate area. Network partitioning is a significant weakness in these protocols that prevents messages from being transmitted on time.

- Robust Vehicular Routing (ROVER) protocol: This protocol uses the flooding approach to send control packets. On the other hand, data messages are sent via Unicast. This protocol separates the network into key components. A car will only accept a message after that if it is received when it is there.

1.8.6 Broadcast-Based Routing Protocols

Broadcasting is the process of sending data packets from one node to all others in the network. This strategy is often employed in cases when it is deemed more efficient or necessary to provide information to all nodes, such as in WSNs. However, this behavior may cause increased network congestion and scalability issues.

The position-aware reliable broadcasting protocol and density-aware reliable broadcasting protocol are intended to assure the reliable distribution of information in wireless networks [60]. Conventional methods for information routing across VANETs are said to rely on flooding-based broadcast routing techniques. Vehicles outside the communication range of the source node can utilize these protocols to share information about emergencies and road conditions. Every network node receives and sends packets under all circumstances.

- BROADCOMM: This method is used to construct cells in the area. Each member of the cell then selects the cell reflector. The cell either gathers signals from neighboring nodes or reflects them. In short, all other nodes will use the cell reflector as their Base Station (BS). As a result, a cell reflector will send messages to other vehicular nodes within the cell.

1.9 ROUTING STRATEGIES

In VANETs, the routing strategy is a critical component that is responsible for establishing and maintaining continuous pathways between source and destination nodes. The routing protocols are solely responsible for maintaining and controlling all of these different services. Routing strategies have a considerable impact on VANET network functioning [61]. Routing protocols may be divided into routing information techniques and route discovery depending on their routing strategies.

1.9.1 Routing Information Approaches

The use of routing information techniques is critical in ensuring the efficient operation of networks, particularly VANETs. Some of the common components associated with routing information are:

- The routing table is a basic data structure used in networking to store information about available routes to various destinations within a network. The routing table is critical to router functioning because it allows them to determine the most effective path for sending packets to their intended destinations [62].
    a. Network administrators create and configure static routing tables. These tables are used to provide a predefined route for data transmission between a certain source and destination. Static routing is well-known for its inherent

simplicity; nonetheless, it lacks flexibility when confronted with changing situations [63].

b. Dynamic routing tables: These tables allow routers to acquire and change routing information autonomously, making them an important component of network architecture. Dynamic routing protocols like Routing Information Protocol (RIP), Open Shortest Path First (OSPF), and Border Gateway Protocol (BGP) enable this [64]. These protocols enable routers to continuously acquire and modify routing information, ensuring efficient and reliable data transmission throughout a network. This enables networks to react adaptively to changes in network design and traffic characteristics.

- The hop count is an important statistic used in routing algorithms to determine the number of intermediate devices (hops) between the origin and destination. The measure of hop count is often used in shortest-path methods.
- Routing algorithms in computer networks determine the most effective path for data packets from a source node to a destination [65].
- The term convergence time refers to how long it takes routers to update their routing tables.

1.9.2 Route Discovery

Route discovery in VANETs entails identifying a suitable route that connects a source vehicle to a destination vehicle or infrastructure component. To properly handle the unique difficulties provided by vehicular settings, existing routing algorithms must be modified to meet the dynamic and rapidly changing nature of VANETs [66]. The procedures of beaconing and route finding are critical in the context of route discovery. Vehicles send out beacon signals on occasion to notify others of their presence and provide critical information such as their current position, speed, and direction. Automobiles may detect and connect to other cars in their near proximity by using these beacon signals, resulting in a bendable and ad hoc network.

1.9.3 Routing Procedure

Routing is a basic function that identifies the most effective path to convey data from the source to the desired destination. The routing network architecture consists of several protocols, methods, and processes designed expressly to allow the efficient transportation of data packets across a network [67]. The following are critical components of the routing network architecture:

- Routing protocols: A set of rules that govern how routers communicate with one another. This connection allows for the sharing of crucial knowledge about the network's state and the discovery of appropriate paths for sending data from its source to its intended destination. Routing tables in routers primarily serve this purpose. These tables include critical information on the network's design, accessible routes, and the most efficient ways to reach certain destinations.
- Routers use routing algorithms to optimize data packet delivery from source to destination inside a computer network. The goal of a routing algorithm is to make correct decisions about the most efficient pathways within a network while taking into consideration a variety of criteria, such as network design and network circumstances.
- Routing metrics: Quantities given to variables influencing network routing. These criteria help routers choose the best path for transmitting data packets from source to destination. Different routing protocols and algorithms use distinct metrics to determine the most efficient routes while taking into account the network's current status [68].
- QoS: It refers to a variety of methodologies and technologies developed to efficiently control and enhance network performance, dependability, and efficiency. Techniques are used to provide preference to certain applications or data flows. Prioritization allows for optimizing the network resources, resulting in increased efficiency and a more consistent and dependable user experience. QoS is especially important in network contexts where many forms of traffic, such as audio, video, and data, compete for limited bandwidth resources [69].

1.10 ROUTING CHALLENGES IN VANET

Traditional routing protocols cause several problems when used directly for VANET routing. In a metropolitan situation, immense buildings and trees prohibit direct connection between cars, increasing message transmission time. GPS does not operate in tunnels, which affects position-based routing systems. Topology-based routing methods add overhead since they need a route-finding mechanism. It uses more bandwidth, delivers duplicate packets, and does not notify of connection failure [70].

Due to the enormous number of automobiles in the city, multi-hop routing causes increased latency and packet loss. The probability of picking a route when more than one option is available decreases as network disruption occurs.

The existence of misbehaving nodes reduces the security of information sharing. Routing in VANET has several issues. The following outline highlights some of the significant challenges:

- Scalability refers to a network's ability to manage increasing numbers of nodes. Scalability is greater in rural locations due to the low population density and the widespread support for conventional routing protocols [71]. Such protocols are ineffective for high-density virtual networks.
- The network's complexity requires additional procedures to find the optimum route between source and destination for packet delivery. The computational cost of a high-dynamic network is higher owing to the longer execution time and the need for significant amounts of memory to maintain routing tables [72]. Traditional routing techniques take longer to select a route because the network changes so quickly.
- Self-organized and adaptable routing refers to autonomous routing, which requires no human involvement. Traditional routing methods demand human involvement anytime network changes occur [73].
- Routing robustness refers to the capacity to maintain a reliable route between source and destination in the event of a connection breakdown.

1.11 SATELLITE RECEIVE ONLY TERMINALS FOR INTERNET ACCESS

The Satellite Receive Only Terminals (SROTs) are a type of ground-based terminal that are specifically designed to receive signals emitted by communication satellites. These terminals are necessary to serve Internet access in remote or underserved locations where it would be otherwise impossible to deploy terrestrial broadband infrastructure (fiber-optic cable or Digital Subscriber Line (DSL)). A traditional SROT system consists of a small parabolic dish (antenna), a low-noise block down converter, and a special receiver unit. The system receives high-frequency signals that are released by satellites in the geostationary or low-Earth orbit and transforms them into useful data streams for the Internet.

Therefore, when no data is being sent, the end users will be forced to use other uplink channels, like telephone or mobile telecommunications, to submit requests or transfer information to the wider Internet.

SROTs are also often used with composite satellite-terrestrial network designs to provide Internet access. Upon a request, e.g., loading a webpage, the request is sent via a low-bandwidth uplink, normally by a terrestrial medium, with the content sent by the satellite downlink to the receive-only receiver. This asymmetric design is specifically suited when the traffic contains a high percentage of large downloads and small uploads, as seen when browsing the web, video streaming, and file downloading. The major advantages of SROTs involve a broad geographical area coverage, a shorter deployment timeframe, and improved usability in geographically remote areas. On the other hand, weaknesses include a longer propagation delay due to the longer distance between the satellite and the Earth, vulnerability to weather-induced signal degradation, and the need to have a different uplink band.

1.12 INTERNET ACCESS TO VANET VIA SATELLITE RECEIVE ONLY TERMINALS

Communication, particularly Internet access, is a fundamental need in contemporary productive settings. Traveling between locations via automobiles consumes a significant amount of time; this duration may be more productive if we have Internet connectivity. A lot of research has been done regarding the Internet integration in vehicles using three main modalities, namely: (1) Internet access only using RSUs or with V2V communications, (2) Internet access using cellular networks, and (3) Internet access using satellite (both symmetric and asymmetric).

There are certain barriers to each modality. Roadside Internet access requires extensive use of RSUs to achieve coverage; the typical radius of the coverage of an RSU is about 250 meters, which means that every 400 to 500 meters, therefore, RSUs should be connected to the Internet, which is expensive to construct, connect, and maintain. The required connectivity is especially hard to achieve in the early phases of VANET implementation and in the countryside or on highways. Access to the internet through cellular networks is slower and therefore more expensive per bit than other solutions.

Cellular networks, which are structured based on the statistical features of call traffic, are contrastingly different from the features of Internet utilization. In addition, their idiosyncratic infrastructure does not take advantage of the asymmetry of Internet traffic.

As a result, it is likely that cellular systems will have difficulties in supporting large amounts of data, particularly when the total population of vehicles in a single cell is all using the Internet at the same time. As a vehicle goes across international borders, service providers and carrier frequencies may often change, resulting in higher costs and complexity of user equipment. Having multiple service providers creates various gateways, along with complications related to billing and licensing. Accessing the Internet by symmetric satellite necessitates that cars be outfitted with satellite transceivers, hence increasing the cost of user equipment.

The satellite channel experiences significant losses, which result in transmission problems necessitating error-correcting methods. These restrictions have a particularly severe effect in densely populated cities with numerous structures and other man-made constructions. Based on this, satellite Internet connectivity cannot be considered a cost-effective option in urban areas. The nature of internet traffic and many of the possible VANET applications are characterized by a strongly asymmetric nature, with downlink traffic taking on orders of magnitude greater value than the uplink traffic. Such an imbalance will continue to increase as more of the content takes the form of multimedia. Satellite downlinks with terrestrial low-bandwidth return media like dial-up have delivered Internet access to home users (at least in rural regions) for longer durations in the past.

Consequently, asymmetric satellite communication, which only offers downlink, has been embraced. The application of satellites in connectivity in rural areas seems to be valid, since it minimizes the loss incurred and the resulting error in the areas or highways. Uplink traffic is based on the roadside infrastructure, based on V2I communication or V2V combined with V2I. However, the number of RSUs is low, making traditional asymmetric satellite solutions impossible. The main problem of VANETs is that the terrestrial return channel is not always available, and it can be severely disrupted, especially at early stages of implementation.

1.13 POSITION-BASED ROUTING USING INTERNET ACCESS TO VANET VIA SATELLITE RECEIVE ONLY TERMINALS

The concept of position-based routing and the use of SROT as the means of Internet access in VANETs is an innovative method of implementing Internet connectivity in smart transport networks to make the transport system more efficient. VANETs enable real-time exchange of vehicular information (position, velocity, and traffic conditions) and thus aid collision avoidance applications, traffic control applications, and path-planning applications. In infrastructural-hazardous areas, like remote areas where the RSUs and the cellular network are inadequate, it is difficult to have continuity of connection. Use of satellite communication through SROTs is an effective way to go since it ensures that even in the case that a terrestrial network is not available, the worldwide data reception is still guaranteed.

In this architecture, vehicles utilize position-based routing protocols that make routing decisions based on the geographic locations of the nodes, while the SROTs serve as a gateway for receiving real-time Internet information via satellite communication. This design allows the vehicles to use important Internet-based features such as cloud-based navigation, weather information, and traffic data broadcasting without having a complete satellite transceiver. As a result, the solution reduces the reliance on traditional infrastructure and improves the trustworthiness of the information sharing in low-density settings. Hence, the development of position-based routing and satellite-based Internet access through SROTs significantly increases the communication resilience, safety, and information accessibility in VANET ecosystems.

1.14 NETWORK SIMULATOR

This section relates to the NS-3 Simulator. This thesis will provide an overview of the NS-3, including its development process, architecture, applications, and installation instructions. Custom scripts will be used to test different routing protocols.

1.14.1 Introduction to NS3

As a free program published under the GNU General Public License version 2, NS-3, also known as Network Simulation 3, is a discrete event network simulator that is the successor to NS-2 and is mainly intended for use in research and teaching. Thus, a license was developed to ensure that the software may be freely shared or altered, which is important for any researcher who plans to utilize and alter the NS-3 for their study.

Since it should be in line with the simulation requirements of current networking research that is developed with the encouragement and contribution of the community, primarily established by students and researchers, the NS-3 project is one of the few reference projects of an open-source simulator for an extensible network simulation platform for networking research and education. From simulation configurations to performance analysis of real-time network emulators that could be connected to the real world, because it enables many existing real-world protocol implementations to be used in NS-3 simulations, these contributors seek to establish a strong simulation core for the NS-3 project that is well-documented and meets the needs of the entire simulation workflow. These can be found in the following GitLab repository: https://gitlab.com/nsnam.

Thus, NS-3 offers a simulation engine core that facilitates the study of both IP-based and non-IP-based networks, providing models of how packet data networks function. This capability allows researchers to investigate network behavior in a controlled and repeatable setting, enabling studies that would be difficult or impossible to conduct in actual networks.

1.14.2 Structure of NS3

The NS-3 simulator is a C++ library that offers a collection of network simulation models wrapped in Python and implemented as C++ objects. As a result, to utilize this library, the application has to be written in Python or C++ to instantiate a collection of simulation models to configure and execute the desired simulation scenario.

The pybindgen library wraps the NS-3 library in Python, enabling users to interact with its modules and core using Python scripts. This means that the NS-3 C++ headers are parsed by gccxml and pygccxml to create the corresponding C++ files that are compiled into the NS-3 Python module.

NS-3 stands apart from the majority of other discrete-event simulators due to its high-level architecture. As we will see in greater detail in the coming sections, NS-3 simulates events using simple function calls that are scheduled to run at a specified simulation time. This means that a callback function can be used to schedule any function as an event, allowing each event to call and activate other events.

1.14.3 NS3 Installation & Setup

Given that NS-3 primarily develops on GNU/Linux platforms, we recommend using the Linux environment due to its reliability. The NS-3 emulator is available on Linux, Mac OS, and even Microsoft Windows via Cygwin. Consequently, this part will provide a concise tutorial on how to install NS-3 on the Ubuntu Linux distribution. However, some requirements must be met before NS-3 may be installed. These requirements result from NS-3 libraries, which rely on third-party libraries like C++ and Python, among others.

1.15 SUMO SIMULATOR

The Simulation of Urban MObility (SUMO) simulator is the subject of this section. For this thesis, it will provide an overview of SUMO, including what it is, how it is developed, its architecture, applications, and installation instructions. Lastly, it will explain how to design unique mobility scenarios for testing the different routing protocols.

1.15.1 Introduction to SUMO

The primary goals of SUMO, a free and open-source vehicle traffic simulation, are research, teaching, and business. Development of the Simulation of Urban Mobility (SUMO) is the major task of the staff of the German Aerospace Center (DLR) and is released under the Eclipse Public License Version 2.0. Such a licensing model ensures that the program can be shared and modified at no cost as long as the source code is open. Since its first publication in 2001, SUMO has made it possible to perform model traffic networks comprising pedestrians, public transport, and private vehicles. The tool suite uses a vast assortment of additional utility tools that are used to automate the necessary processes in the development, execution, and analysis of traffic simulators, e.g., network import, route calculations, visualization, and analysis of emissions. Moreover, SUMO provides various Application Programming Interfaces (APIs) and capabilities to make the simulation more realistic and applicable, and may be customized with custom models.

1.15.2 Applications of SUMO

One of the major contributions to various areas of research is the fact that SUMO stands out in its field due to its high sense of realism and advanced simulation abilities. There is a great number of initiatives, research, and real-life applications that have used SUMO to understand phenomena in transport. The list of several applications that SUMO has had is as follows:

- The Vehicle-to-Everything (V2X) community uses SUMO extensively for both providing realistic vehicle traces and evaluating applications in an online loop with a network simulator.
- Vehicle route choice has been studied, including the development of new methods, the evaluation of eco-aware routing based on pollutant emissions, and investigations into the network-wide influences of autonomous route choice.
- Traffic light performance evaluation includes the evaluation of contemporary algorithms up to the evaluation of weekly timing plans.
- AI trains traffic light plans.
- The impact of platoons and driverless cars on traffic is simulated.
- Working with other simulators, the autonomous driving function is simulated and validated.
- Parking traffic simulation.
- The simulator also performs risk analysis and ensures traffic safety.
- The system also calculates emissions, including pollutants and noise.

1.15.3 SUMO Installation & Setup

The three primary Operating Systems (OS) environments—Windows, Linux, and even Mac OS—all support the SUMO simulator. Both Linux and Windows versions, in my experience, function reliably and effectively. However, as Linux is where the NS-3 simulator is most reliable and where this thesis's experimental portion is completed, it is advised to utilize it there. Thus, utilizing the Git repositories that include all of the binary Linux versions of SUMO, this section will provide a quick overview of the SUMO simulator and its primary tools for Linux. Like NS-3, the SUMO simulator also needs some prerequisites, including CMake, Python, and g++, among others, for various SUMO utilities.

1.16 COUPLING ARCHITECTURE OF SUMO & NS3

Anyone may create realistic mobility situations for the study of VANET routing protocols by combining the two applications, SUMO and NS3, using the SUMO&NS3-Coupling tool. The tool accomplishes this by guiding the user through a series of steps seamlessly and sequentially. The procedure may be broken down into the following four stages:

- Development of Vehicle Mobility Scenarios: In this first stage, we develop the mobility scenarios. To begin with the SUMO&NS3 coupling, we require the mobility files from the SUMO simulator.
- The second step is called "SUMO&NS3-Coupling Translation," in which the user enters mobility files into the SUMO&NS3-Coupling tool. This allows the software to function until all results are produced. Similar to a translation process from SUMO to NS3, the application takes the input mobility files, parses them, and then automatically generates new files that the NS3 may consume.
- The third step is called "NS3 Simulation," in which the NS3 simulator uses the translated mobility files to begin simulating network traffic using various routing protocols, including AODV, OLSR, and DSDV, operating in a WAVE environment. Following each run with the various simulators, output data is produced and sent back to the SUMO&NS3-Coupling.
- SUMO&NS3-Coupling Results: This final phase involves the SUMO&NS3-Coupling, taking the output from the NS3 simulator, primarily consisting of .csv data, and automatically performing statistical analysis on it while also generating graphs to better visualize the Key Performance Indicators (KPIs) of the simulated scenarios.

1.17 PROBLEM IDENTIFICATION AND MOTIVATION

Driving becomes increasingly risky and demanding in the early stages due to increased traffic congestion, injuries, and deaths. To prevent this, the automobile maker works with government agencies to research and create a solution to assist drivers on the road by forecasting important events or impacted traffic areas. The result leads to the development of a revolutionary wireless technology known as WAVE, which is utilized for V2V and V2I communication. WAVE enables ITSs that include traffic monitoring, vehicle navigation, collision avoidance, traffic congestion management, and traffic signal control, as well as driver and passenger information. To ensure the safety of drivers and passengers, the sharing of information (both safe and unsafe) necessitates the development of intelligent and efficient routing protocols. These procedures should enable independent decisions in emergency scenarios. To regulate continuous multi-hop routing, routing protocols may be classified as position-based, topology-based, broadcast-based, multicast, cluster-based, and so on.

Several studies show that with typical routing algorithms, the throughput for each VANET decreases dramatically as the number of nodes increases. Furthermore, the usage of flat and conventional routing in automotive networks results in poor scalability and communication dependability. As a result, effective routing systems have been designed with two crucial qualities in mind: scalability and dependability. Thus, a cluster-based routing protocol has been proposed to promote scalability, while a multipath technique has been created to improve reliability in vehicular communication. This aids in determining the shortest route by reacting more effectively to the changing topology of VANETs.

Message exchange between cars using VANETs may assist in avoiding traffic congestion, making travel more pleasant and safe for the driver and co-travelers. The main criterion for successful communication in VANETs is to use a routing algorithm that reduces latency while increasing Packet Delivery Ratio (PDR) and throughput. Thereby, this research seeks to build and implement a position-based routing protocol in VANETs by providing an internet connection to VANET using satellite receive-only terminals.

1.18 STATEMENT OF THE PROBLEM

The high mobility of vehicles presents an unresolved research challenge about the applicability of traditional routing protocols to address issues related to this mobility. This research will address the following issues:

- Reliable communication is very difficult with VANETs due to their high mobility and frequent topology changes. Because of their high node mobility and quick topology changes, VANETs struggle to sustain dependable communication.
- Traditional routing and MAC-layer protocols struggle to adapt to dynamic circumstances, resulting in poor performance under high mobility or heavy traffic.
- Expanding internet access to VANETs requires considerable roadside infrastructure, which may be challenging during the initial stages of building vehicle networks or in places with insufficient infrastructure.
- RSU implementation is limited in rural regions and along roads due to high costs and inadequate infrastructure, resulting in communication disruptions.

1.19 OBJECTIVES

The primary goal of this study is to improve the performance and reliability of routing protocols in VANETs by using location prediction and adaptive transmission techniques. The particular interim objectives include:

- To enhance PDR by reducing connection disruptions resulting from fast node mobility and dynamic topology changes. Also enhancing the dependability of routing protocols by real-time position forecasting and adaptive regulation of transmission power, connection quality, and queue status.
- To minimize E2E delivery latency by proactively picking stable routes based on anticipated locations and network conditions. Additionally, decrease the frequency of packet retransmissions by using predictive routing and adjusting transmission power, therefore alleviating congestion and minimizing collisions.
- To concurrently enhance energy efficiency, QoS, and flexibility for diverse mobility models and traffic circumstances in VANETs. Facilitate internet access for automobile systems, especially during the initial installation phase and in areas with little roadside connection.
- To improve VANET connection in low-density RSU networks and ensure communication reliability in sparse RSU environments.

1.20 PROPOSED SOLUTION

The proposed solutions of this research are the following:

- The first contribution proposes a hybrid system that uses a position prediction module and Adaptive Transmission Control Protocol (ATCP) to improve routing in VANETs, resulting in greater PDR, reduced E2E latency, and improved network quality.
- The second contribution suggests a unique cross-layer protocol, Federated Deep Reinforcement Learning with Graph Neural Networks (Fed-GNN-DRL), for achieving energy-aware and QoS-guaranteed communication in VANETs. It generates vehicular topology graphs using location and mobility data, which are encoded using lightweight GNNs. It employs a dual-timescale DRL agent to optimize both fast-timescale MAC settings and slow-timescale network operations.

It guarantees that policies are constantly updated to account for changes in traffic and mobility.

- The third contribution proposes a strategy that complements existing ones while eliminating the necessity for fully networked roadside infrastructure. To offer extensive Internet connectivity, this technique uses satellite receive-only endpoints and a limited number of (distributed) roadside devices.
- The fourth contribution proposes an enhanced Dynamic Source Routing (DSR) protocol that uses satellite-assisted communication to address connection concerns. This protocol investigates the quality of DSR in virtual scenarios of sparse RSU utilization, using measures such as PDR, network speed, E2E latency, and route stability.
- The fifth contribution introduces a new hybrid routing system using the Ọdịgbo Metaheuristic Optimization Algorithm (OMOA). This protocol improves routing efficiency and reliability by using metaheuristic optimization, machine learning-based route scoring, and probabilistic filtering.

1.21 ORGANIZATION OF THE THESIS

The thesis is organized as follows:

Chapter 1 provides background information for this study. It provides an overview of VANET's infrastructure, components, features, applications, and problems. It also examines routing, the taxonomy of routing protocols, and the issues they face in VANETs. It also defines the network simulation environment for VANETs.

Chapter 2 provides a thorough examination of the current routing protocols in VANETs.

Chapter 3 introduces the ATCP with a position prediction approach for reliable and scalable routing in VANETs. The performance of this framework is also evaluated by comparing it to other similar systems.

Chapter 4 presents the novel Fed-GNN-DRL model, which serves as an energy-efficient and QoS-guaranteed routing protocol in VANETs. It also compares the efficacy of this approach to similar ones.

Chapter 5 describes position-based routing using Internet interface to VANET via a satellite receive-only terminal. The performance of this protocol is also evaluated and compared to other VANET protocols.

Chapter 6 evaluates and enhances VANET connections in sparse RSU situations using an upgraded DSR protocol. It also compares the efficacy of this protocol to that of other relevant protocols.

Chapter 7 introduces a novel OMOA-based routing protocol for VANETs, focusing on energy efficiency and reliability. It also compares the efficacy of this approach to other ones.

Chapter 8 presents the research's conclusion, including simulation data.

Chapter 9 outlines the extent of future effort related to the recommended solutions.

CHAPTER 2

LITERATURE SURVEY

2.1 INTRODUCTION

VANET has garnered increasing attention over the years within the context of ITS, presenting a possible option for the Car-To-Car Communication Consortium (C2C-CC). Various nations globally are currently conducting diverse VANET analyses and regulatory initiatives. The PReVENT initiative in Europe, co-sponsored by the European transmission contract, seeks to improve highway safety and formulate preventive measures within the European automobile sector. In the United States (US), the Vehicle Safety Communications Consortium (VSCC) is actively participating in similar activities. The ITS Consortium and the advanced safety vehicle initiative in Japan are focused on enhancing safety via technology.

In 2006, General Motors demonstrated V2V deployment with Cadillac vehicles, while other automotive manufacturers such as BMW, Toyota, Daimler, Audi, Volvo, Honda, and the C2C-CC are involved in V2V interaction initiatives. Notwithstanding the capacity for efficient labor, traffic congestion is anticipated to increase, with road fatalities predicted to rank as the fifth leading cause of death by 2030. The prediction indicates that the worldwide market value of connected cars is anticipated to reach $225,160 million, a substantial rise from $63,026 million in 2017, with an annual growth rate of 17.1% from 2020 to 2027. Consequently, a dependable, effective, and secure communication system is required to provide real-time communication between vehicles, along with value-added services. VANET has attracted interest from both academics and businesses for facilitating secure communication that satisfies security and privacy standards. Furthermore, reducing latency and maintaining acceptable communication overhead is essential for VANET connectivity.

Routing protocols in VANETs are essential for ensuring reliable data transmission amidst challenges like high mobility, frequent topology changes, and varying traffic densities. These protocols can be broadly classified into topology-based, position-based, cluster-based, and bio-inspired. Hybrid approaches often combine these paradigms to optimize performance, incorporating elements like machine learning for predictive routing or traffic awareness to minimize delays.

The choice of protocol significantly impacts network efficiency, with position-based and bio-inspired methods showing promise in urban scenarios due to their adaptability to real-time conditions. This chapter provides a comprehensive literature survey on the evolution and advancements in VANET routing protocols, drawing from a wide array of studies spanning from early developments to recent innovations incorporating bio-inspired algorithms, clustering techniques, traffic-aware mechanisms, geographic positioning, and deep learning approaches. The survey is structured to cover key categories of routing protocols for V2V, V2I, and hybrid communications, highlighting their strengths, limitations, and performance metrics such as PDR, E2E latency, throughput, and overhead.

2.2 ROUTING PROTOCOLS FOR V2V COMMUNICATION

In [74], an overview of routing protocols and associated mobility models for VANETs was provided. Position-based [75], location-based [76], reactive location-based [77], and topology-based [78] routing protocols were described for V2V scenarios. A summary of the benefits and drawbacks of VANET position-based routing protocol advancements may be found in [79]. In [80, 81], the authors provided the performance study of routing protocols for V2V communication in city settings. Ad-hoc On-demand Multipath Distance Vector Routing (AOMDV) and AODV were the reactive protocols that were assessed, while DSDV was the proactive protocol. According to the investigation, reactive routing techniques were more effective at maintaining the connection via recurring information exchange, which is essential for TCP-based traffic.

In [82, 83], the authors provided improved AODV routing protocols in VANETs, where optimization was carried out based on choosing the route procedure to improve route stability and reduce overhead. It performs better in terms of connection reliability and PDR. In [84], an AODV-based rapid route recovery technique for V2V communication was introduced. Every time the connection breaks, the basic AODV was changed. When the connection fails, it determines the target vehicle's heading and notifies the cars in its vicinity to locate an alternate route. During its route discovery phase, Speed and Direction-based AOMDV (SD-AOMDV), another advancement in AODV, determines the next hop [85]. Cluster-based routing protocol types were examined in [86] according to different vehicle parameters, advantages, disadvantages, and problems encountered during implementation.

In [87], a minimal delay routing protocol was presented that computes the latency for its intermediate cars by taking into account the neighbor vehicle's speed and distance from the destination. The Traffic Flow-Oriented Routing (TFOR) protocol for VANETs was the subject of discussion in [88]. Roads with several lanes and opposing directions were considered in real-time urban settings. This reduces E2E latency and increases the PDR.

An extension of the AODV+ routing system, M-AODV+ (Modified AODV+), was described in [89]. When intermediate nodes cannot be located, the connections within vehicles were enabled to allow V2V communication consistency. A fixed hotspot is at the heart of the Routing-Tree-based Data Forwarding (RTDF) dynamic routing method for road networks, which was introduced in [90]. When several queries were received in a vehicle at once, this will transmit information to create a route tree for message delivery. A multihop dependable and effective broadcast routing technique for VANETs was introduced in [91] and is based on relative speed and mobility prediction.

The core AODV routing protocol of VANET incorporates a dependable communication model known as AODV-R, which is detailed in [92], because of the frequent changes in network topology caused by high velocity. Depending on the direction, location, and speed of the vehicles on the route, the system determines the connection between them. Routing protocols based on video applications were examined in [93, 94].

In [95], link assessment techniques for V2V and V2I were introduced. Using the NS3 simulator, the performance of location, cross-layer, and prediction-related protocols was examined while taking into account the different Link Estimation Techniques (LETs) characteristics, including distance, speed, and Signal-to-Noise Rate (SNR). When compared to the other VANET routing protocols, the cross-layer protocol performed better.

To choose the next crossing on the road to transfer data packets, Real-Time Intersection-based road Segment-Aware Routing (RTISAR) [96] uses the road segment status based on load segment, connection, density, and total distance to the destination. In the event of link connection or disconnection, the routing mechanism takes into account both historical and real-time traffic circumstances, as detailed in [97].

2.3 ROUTING PROTOCOLS FOR V2I COMMUNICATION

In [98], routing systems for V2V and V2I communication were discussed along with their benefits and drawbacks. In [99], a routing scheme based on a distributed clustering algorithm in the vehicle-to-infrastructure (V2I) mode is introduced. V2I communications allow continuous safety and entertainment applications, as mentioned in [100-102].

Machine learning is one of the subfields of artificial intelligence that helps to acquire knowledge and train the model without any human intervention or explicit programming. A deep reinforcement learning (DRL) approach in [103] outlines the necessary data to route vehicles to anything (VANET) in a V2I setup. The DRA framework predicts the data packets of vehicle mobility and paths, respectively. In densely populated urban settings, co-channel interference appears to be the greatest problem [104, 105].

In [106], a VANET cell-based V2I scenario is presented, in which the cell is used to define a congested urban environment based on the Manhattan mobility model, in that there are multiple lanes located on the cell boundary, thus causing an important amount of Co-Channel Interference (CCI). The Coordinated Multipoint (CoMP) transmission and active Inter-Cell Interference Coordination (ICIC) methods are implemented to improve the reliability of communication. Several performance metrics, including received interference and the mean throughput of the vehicle user, were used to estimate these techniques.

2.4 ROUTING PROTOCOLS FOR HYBRID COMMUNICATION

A hybrid routing system was anticipated in urban areas with automobiles and buses [107]. To enhance the network's overall performance, it employs the store-carry-and-forward technique and the greedy forwarding approach. In [108, 109], a central routing concept was explained that uses an AI-based Software Defined Network (SDN) controller to forecast vehicle activity and decrease VANET latency. Switches use network information gathered from RSUs to determine the best pathways to reduce the vehicle's total operating delay. In [110], the fish swarm method was introduced to provide a dependable connection for hybrid networks. Based on the prey behavior of a swarm of fish, a path was constructed for both city and highway situations using the location of the vehicle. Trust between vehicles was essential to ITS safety and security strategies.

The security techniques used in VANET to enable the safe flow of data include authenticity, availability, integrity, and secrecy [111, 112]. Routing relies on the number of hops and the reliability of the path to determine the best route for sending a dependable message [113, 114]. Cars' self-centered behavior, which manifests as packet dropping, decreases network efficiency. An effective plan for disconnected delay-tolerant VANETs was provided in [115] to address this problem. In [116], it was addressed how cooperative and noncooperative game theory might be used to handle security challenges at the network layer.

2.5 REVIEW ON ROUTING PROTOCOLS FOR VANET

2.5.1 Bio-Inspired Routing Protocols

Ramamoorthy and Thangavelu [117] suggested that due to rapid movement and topological changes, communication links in VANETs between vehicles are susceptible to frequent failures. An Enhanced Bio-Inspired Routing Algorithm (EBIRA) was presented to provide reliable communication. In EBIRA, the optimal short-distance routes with few hops were determined using Enhanced Ant Colony Optimization (EACO), which relies on distance, received signal strength metrics, hop count, and evaporation rate. The chosen route in EBIRA was concise and exhibited a significant degree of link-level connectivity with few hops. The EBIRA route finding success ratio was assessed in conjunction with variations in received signal intensity, which depend on vehicle density and speed.

Soni [118] suggested that the developed approach improved throughput, packet size, and overhead with reduced time. The testing findings validated that, in comparison to other algorithms in the simulation, the developed method provided superior packet size and throughput while exhibiting reduced latency and overhead. Abbas et al. [119] emphasized the need to enhance network efficiency in VANETs due to the high dynamic mobility on roads. An effective routing system was essential to ensure that cars reach their destination in the shortest feasible period.

Gopalakrishnan et al. [120] proposed a bio-inspired routing protocol to identify the optimal gateway and sink for routing service requests between the service requester and the global server. The gateway decision aimed to facilitate communication exclusively with the authentic source before reaching the sink. The networking nodes were provided with efficient routing. The VANET sources used software-defined networking to stabilize the networking topologies.

Liu et al. [121] presented a Parking-Area-Assisted Spider-Web Routing Protocol (PASRP) for emergency data in urban VANETs. A digital map and geographic information system were used to develop a parking lot-oriented spider-web transmission system. The emergency information was then sent on the designated channel via a multi-mode greedy algorithm. The data were prioritized via a dynamic multi-priority scheduling methodology. The simulation results indicated that the proposed approach surpassed traditional procedures.

Yelure et al. [122] created a Particle Swarm Optimization based Routing (PSOR) routing approach with PSO for VANET, which improved QoS. The particle's velocity and location were used to verify the optimal solution based on fitness value. The subsequent car that was accessible near the destination vehicle was chosen using this strategy. The message was conveyed via the carry and forward technique. The testing results verified that, in comparison to other algorithms in the simulation, the developed method provided superior packet size and throughput, along with reduced latency and overhead.

Tian et al. [123] suggested using cellular attractor selection to determine subsequent hops for VANET. This algorithm emphasized the significance of adapting to its intricate and evolving surroundings. Furthermore, the selection of the next hop using a multi-attribute decision-making process resulted in a reduction of duplicate candidates. The simulation results indicated that the proposed technique outperformed the existing strategy for PDR, E2E latency, and congestion. The authors introduced the Genetic Algorithm with Ant Colony Optimization (GAACO) approach in [124], enabling cars to communicate with each other in varying traffic volumes. They tested their suggested framework in Dehradun, India. They claimed that intersatellite communications might also make use of this protocol.

Khan and colleagues [125] presented an inventive method for implementing the Internet of energy within the context of a bus-based VANET architecture. To overcome the difficulties involved in relay bus selection and traffic route optimization, the authors' algorithm used a street-centric routing philosophy. This work aimed to develop a multipath routing algorithm that takes into account the likelihood of street and path regularity. Performance was shown to be improved by using multipath routing approaches in terms of PDR and E2E latency, or the time it takes for data to move from its starting point to its final destination. The development of a unique clustering-based method for selecting relay buses that also utilizes ACO was another recommendation given to improve the packet forwarding process. The main goal of the relay bus's development was to improve the quality of packets sent to the next forwarding relay. Based on the investigation's findings, it was found that using clustering in combination with the ACO approach improves the selection process for relay buses. The system saw notable improvements with reduced latency from start to finish, lower computation costs, and the removal of unnecessary beacon signals.

Datta et al. [126] introduced ant-AODV-VANET, an innovative routing protocol that integrates the concepts of ACO into the framework of VANETs. The results validated the prediction that the most efficient route, defined by the shortest distance and superior connection quality, would provide the most advantageous consequences. The results showed that the route identified by the proposed technique displays much more accuracy than an alternative method.

Murugan et al. [127] performed simulations using PSO and ACO algorithms, applying performance indicators like PDR, latency, throughput, goodput, packet drop, and dropping ratio. With the increasing rise in automotive traffic in urban regions, it has become important to maximize the use of existing resources to reduce the load on infrastructure and limit energy consumption. The reduction of network traffic and the use of load-balancing measures aided in alleviating the drop. The use of ACO and PSO was evaluated to identify the most reliable path, hence reducing the probability of connection failures in a designated geographical region, while also demonstrating enhanced responsiveness to changes in the network structure.

Sasirekha et al. [128] proposed a heuristic method designed to reduce network overhead in multi-path ACO algorithms. The main aim of this method was to eliminate nodes anticipated to be the least efficient intermediary nodes inside the VANET framework. The use of the ACO approach was applied to obtain the selection of an optimum route. The findings indicated that the adoption of a route map ACO was an effective method for improving packet transmission efficiency and minimizing network overhead. The proposed technique demonstrates a more favorable equilibrium relative to current methods. Future progress included the use of machine learning methods to assess performance measures.

Othman et al. [129] performed an extensive investigation of the ACO technique to tackle the Vehicle Routing Problem (VRP). The following question pertained to the ACO algorithm. The analysis and execution of the algorithm's objective function were conducted within the context of the VRP. The algorithm's effectiveness was enhanced by decreasing the stopping criteria. The research focused on analyzing control parameters to get the optimal value for each parameter. Subsequent to the development of the control parameters, a comprehensive study was performed to evaluate the efficacy of the ACO algorithm in addressing the VRP. The method's effectiveness is linked to the significance of its parameters, namely the number of ants, alpha, beta, and rho. The trail's significance is represented by the variable alpha, visibility is shown by the variable beta, and pheromone decay is governed by the parameter rho. A comparative analysis of the routes from several iterations was conducted to assess the algorithm's performance. Utilizing optimal control settings, the mean and standard deviation of the 20 runtimes were determined to be 1057.839 km and 25.913 km, respectively. Ultimately, a conclusion is created to succinctly encapsulate the findings of the inquiry.

Patel et al. [130] presented an innovative intelligence approach for QoS multicast routing via a hybrid ACO/PSO algorithm. A proposed multicast tree that satisfies the criteria for latency, delay jitter, bandwidth, and loss rate was developed using the approach. The software amalgamated chosen multicast tree patterns from a collection of randomly generated patterns to construct the multicast tree. The method generated a greater number of patterns and later selected the best suitable ones for creating the multicast tree with precision.

Ranjan Senapati and Mohan Khilar [131] used ACO to provide numerous paths between nodes, an essential element in a network characterized by unpredictable and constantly changing connections. This feature facilitated the simultaneous transmission of packets across many paths, hence decreasing the total delay from the source to the destination. The suggested research sought to examine the relationship between E2E latency, transmission distance, and vehicle count within the framework of VANET routing protocols. They specifically examined the efficacy of two established protocols: Geographical Source Routing (GSR) and Anchor-based Street Traffic Aware Routing (A-STAR). The analysis indicated that the proposed effort exceeds both GSR and A-STAR. The multi-path route solution necessitates the use of MongoDB, an open-source distributed database. The database operation was executed with Node-RED. Choosing an efficient route and intermediate node for transmitting emergency information is very important. The ideal path in VANET seeks to reduce both the overall transmission duration and the E2E latency. To improve route efficiency and minimize intermediate connections in VANET, PSO was used. The aim of this technique was to provide essential information during emergencies with little delay.

Marinaki and Marinakis [132] introduced an innovative hybrid strategy using the Glowworm Swarm Optimization (GSO) algorithm to address the vehicle routing issue with stochastic needs. The vehicle routing problem was categorized as an NP-hard problem. The author developed a novel iteration of the GSO termed Combinatorial Neighborhood Topology

GSO (CNT-GSO). The results of this innovative algorithm were then compared with those of prior variants of the GSO algorithm, as well as with the most effective metaheuristic and evolutionary algorithms, as discussed in the present study. Two specific issues were contrasted: the capacitated vehicle routing problem and the vehicle routing problem with stochastic demands. The implementation of the suggested approach in the Capacitated Vehicle Routing Problem (CVRP) proved to be beneficial as it provided significant insights about the algorithm's performance in the established routing problem. The aim was to ascertain the parameters that yielded the most reliable results.

Chauhan and Dahiya [133] introduced a method that alleviates communication latency resulting from recurrent disconnections in routing. This method linked the ACO metaheuristic search with the AODV routing protocol and provided a route repair strategy for ACO. Agarwal et al. [134] used the ACO Tabu Search (ACOTS) method to minimize the weight of a 25-bar space truss, enhancing its structural design. The distinct values of the bars' cross-sectional areas were the design variables. The numerical analysis of the 25-bar space truss yielded the most optimal, namely the lowest minimum weight value achieved. This instance demonstrated the efficacy and technical feasibility of ACOTS as an optimization approach for discrete-variable optimal structure design. The primary disadvantage of ACO was identified as its prolonged execution time, akin to other modern heuristic combinatorial optimization methods such as simulated annealing, genetic algorithms, and tabu search. The inclusion of the TS local improvement step in ACOTS exacerbated this issue significantly.

Jayachithra et al. [135] demonstrated the efficacy of the ACO algorithm in reducing journey time for an agent navigating a simulated traffic network. The strategy was designed to optimize traffic distribution in a congested network by selecting less busy pathways. The results also indicated that the algorithm exhibited superior performance in a system characterized by substantial traffic congestion. The results were derived via assessing the algorithm's efficacy in circumventing congested routes and minimizing the total trip time inside the network. The definitive results indicated that the ACO algorithm might reduce the journey's duration from 21.13% to 38.99%. The traffic network simulation model was optimized via the ACO approach to identify the best routes. This model exhibited superior performance in a transportation network characterized by substantial congestion levels.

Wang et al. [136] investigated the principal challenge in routing protocols and presented a novel routing approach, ACO-EG, specifically developed for VANETs. The author developed an innovative routing method named JTA-EG, using the concepts of Evolving Graph (EG) theory to investigate connections between two nodes. The ACO-EG algorithm was used to adjust to traffic conditions and identify the optimal route. The performance investigation indicated the potential to improve the PDR while concurrently decreasing E2E latency.

Sumathi and Kumar [137] introduced the Energy-Efficient Perspicacious ACO-Based Routing Protocol (EEPACORP) to reduce latency and energy consumption in MANET. EEPACORP used the inherent traits of ants to effectively categorize and choose the optimal path to a certain goal. EEPACORP adjusted the pheromone concentration to extend the route time, hence improving the network's lifespan. A simulation using NS-3 was conducted to assess the efficacy of EEPACORP relative to other routing protocols. According to the data, EEPACORP achieved a 46.293% decrease in energy usage. EEPACORP might enhance its future direction by integrating various bio-inspired strategies to further decrease energy usage.

Aadil et al. [138] presented Clustering scheme based on ACO for VANET (CACONET). CACONET generated efficient clusters to provide dependable connection. The performance of CACONET was evaluated using empirical technique by comparing it with the leading baseline methodologies, namely Multi-Objective PSO (MOPSO) and Comprehensive Learning PSO (CLPSO). The experiments were also aimed at measuring the relative performance of different algorithms using different grid sizes, the range of node transmission, and the number of nodes in the work group. Clustering optimization was sought through the inclusion of transmission range, directional orientation, and velocity of the node. The empirical evidence indicates that CACONET has better performance when compared to MOPSO and CLPSO.

Kumar and Routray [139] presented one such routing mechanism that combines ACO with DSR. This is driven by the fact that ACO had an enhanced adaptability of routing decisions to a variety of ad hoc network settings, which inspired its adoption. In addition, the mechanism is characterized by such features as dynamic topology processing, link-quality measurement, and route optimality. To manage and control vehicular networks, the authors included vehicular information, like speed and position information, in building an ant-based algorithm that is capable of dynamically adapting to the dynamic nature of vehicular networks. The proposed routes were evaluated using three performance measures, namely, routing overhead, latency, and throughput.

The ACO variant suggested by Manimekala [140] is ACO-PLM, which is a transparent account designed with the purpose of solving the vehicle routing problem. Its methodology relies on the pheromone deployment strategies, a local search, and the use of mutation operators to speed up the convergence. The experimental findings from the twelve benchmark cases and comparative studies with existing algorithms show that ACO-PLM achieves better results than other heuristics.

AntHocNet was an innovative routing protocol designed to suit MANETs [141]. The creation and maintenance of dependable paths in dynamically changing topologies with limited bandwidth is a highly challenging problem, with reliability and efficiency being the chief considerations. AntHocNet is also based on the principles of ant colony optimization and combines both reactive and proactive elements. In the preliminary reactive path construction step, several paths are created within the nodes that are involved in a data session. During the communication process, artificial ants carefully consider prevailing routes and find new ways of pathfinding. According to the simulation studies, AntHocNet outperforms AODV, which is one of the most popular algorithms in the modern world, in terms of E2E latency and PDR.

Belmecheri et al. [142] proposed an ACO approach to address the Heterogeneous Fleet, Mixed Backhauls, and Time Windows (HVRPMBTW) variant of the vehicle routing issue with constraints. This particular variant has received less attention in the existing literature. The primary objective of this study was to include real-world industrial limitations into the scenarios of the VRP. The author conducted a comparative analysis of the outcomes derived from the use of the ACO algorithm. It was shown to be very successful for minor cases, although it did not consistently provide optimum outcomes for more significant problems. Creating a localized search algorithm for ACO that is especially designed to effectively manage enormous issue sizes in the future would be intriguing. Moreover, it was intriguing to devise an alternative and precise methodology to ascertain the absolute minimum criteria.

Deshmukh et al. [143] analyzed the advancements in position-based routing protocols, particularly GPSR and Connectivity Aware Routing (CAR). The used optimization approach was ACO. The CAR and GPSR processes were simulated under two scenarios: with optimization and without optimization. An assessment and comparison of the CAR and GPSR algorithms were performed, emphasizing metrics like average PDR, E2E latency, throughput, routing overhead, and packet loss. The experiment was conducted only using NS-2. The results demonstrated that the use of the ACO methodology enhanced the efficacy of the GPSR and CAR procedures in VANET. Moreover, the CAR therapy shown enhanced results relative to the GPSR approach.

Li and Boukhatem [144] introduced a novel protocol called the Vehicular routing protocol based on ACO (VACO). VACO identified the most effective routing pathways by using the routinely assessed relay quality of road segments. By gathering accurate data at adjacent crossings, the author used the ant colony concept to analyze whole routes connecting the starting and ending intersections. A probabilistic approach using pheromone routing tables guided the path selection at each junction in VACO. The simulation results indicate that the VACO protocol surpassed the GPSR and CAR reference protocols for overhead, average delay, and PDR.

2.5.2 Clustering-Based Routing Protocols

Azhdari et al. proposed a study on VANETs [145]. VANETs pose a routing difficulty because of their features, which include a high degree of node mobility and unpredictable wireless communication connectivity. Additionally, it is essential to develop an authentication technique between the source and destination nodes due to the aforementioned features of these networks. They explained a fuzzy logic-based routing strategy for VANETs that allows authentication. The recommended routing method consists of three components: authentication, routing between CH nodes, and clustering. In the first stage, vehicles are grouped using an efficient technique. In the proposed method, we differentiate between regular and immediate data packets.

Instead of using instantaneous velocity, Ramasamy et al. [146] developed a Position PSO with Fuzzy Logic (PPSO-FL) technique for VANETs that relies on collectively coordinated metrics. A Cluster-based Recursive Broadcast (CRB) routing system was suggested by Dong et al. [147] as a solution to the delivery ratio and delay time problems. Only the chosen vehicles could transmit the received emergency event to other adjacent vehicles. Depending on the traffic light situation, the suggested method enhanced the directed broadcast's message delivery and transmission efficiency. Experiments on NS2 indicated that the suggested method worked better than earlier algorithms.

To increase the stability of the vehicular network and lengthen the linkages between cars, Kandali and Bennis [148] proposed a routing protocol that uses adaptive K-Harmonic Means (RPKHM). The number and beginning positions of the centroids were determined using a mathematical model that considered the structure of the network and the total number of automobiles. In contrast, the data was grouped using a similarity value based on Euclidean distance. In the end, the clusters were kept, and new CHs were chosen based on a cost function that accounted for the Expected Transmission count (ETX) and the overall amount of free buffer. The results of the simulation indicated that the suggested approach was effective in terms of PDR, average E2E time, and throughput.

A reliable cluster-based two-layer method was proposed by Hamedani and Rezazadeh [149] to solve the connection failure problems in VANETs. The first level selected the dependable link, while the second level utilized a greedy algorithm to select the shortest path. The optimal strategy based on network properties like PDR and E2E latency was simulated utilizing NS-2.35 rather than more conventional methods. This method was used to improve both PDR and E2E latency.

To overcome the communication problems with Automated Guided Vehicles (AGVs) and disseminate Mine Detection Messages (MDMs), Farooq et al. [150] created an AAGV routing algorithm that utilized aerial vehicles. To enable the real-time adaptation of the established algorithm without compromising its performance, a cluster-based system was also developed. Reliable Inter-Vehicular Communication (IVC) links were maintained to do this. The NS2 was used to stimulate the established approach. The results demonstrated that by employing a multicast communication strategy, the developed technique increased PDR and throughput while lowering latency and overhead. The study referenced in [151] indicates that the vehicle has improved passenger comfort and traffic safety. Their model hasn't taken security or privacy issues into account.

2.5.3 Traffic-Aware Routing Protocols

According to Gillani et al. [152], VANET research is a difficult but dynamic area of study. ITS provides many uses, including effective road traffic monitoring, efficient traffic flow management, and road safety applications. The predetermined silence segments hinder effective communication during the collection of real-time data for emergencies. Additionally, this problem may result in the postponement of important ITS operations. The proposed real-time Traffic-aware Data Gathering protocol (TDG) employs dynamic segmentation switching to overcome communication limitations. TDG is a dynamic, lightweight system that collects and transmits data packets according to the current and quickly shifting traffic conditions. The primary objective is to minimize network and data transfer overhead to meet real-time data collection time constraints.

An efficient routing protocol for urban VANETs was created in [153]. Several techniques for data packet forwarding within roadways and intersections constitute the Q-learning algorithm [154]. Because of its unique capabilities to handle high vehicle mobility, significant topological changes, and frequent route failures or breaks, VANET has attracted a lot of attention. For metropolitan areas, Goudarzi et al. [155] developed a traffic-aware VANET routing technique. To identify a path with network connectivity, an ant-based method was applied. The optimal path between a source and a destination was identified by comparing the street map route with the least amount of weight for the entire trip when using a source vehicle. To ascertain the precise functionality of the suggested protocol, consideration was given to the simulated environment. According to simulation results, the suggested method was able to improve PDR by 10% while reducing overhead and E2E time at speeds of up to 70 km/h.

Wu [156] presented a map-based, traffic-aware routing system called GeoTAR, in which traffic information was collected and a digital map and the Geohash coding technique were used to identify the best route. Additionally, the Intersection-First Restricted Forwarding (IFRF) restricted forwarding approach was used to forward packets for which structures were considered radio obstacles. The routing path took into account the presence of a wired channel in the RSUs. When compared to alternative protocols, the simulation results indicated that the suggested approach was effective in improving VANET performance in terms of PDR and E2E delay.

For urban VANETs, Wu et al. [157] investigated a novel routing method called Q-learning-based Traffic-Aware Routing (QTAR) based on RSU. To send the packets efficiently, a routing path was employed to select the reliable link road portions. The packet was broadcast in a road segment utilizing distributed V2V Q-learning in conjunction with Q-learning-based Greedy Geographic Forwarding (QGGF) to minimize latency and the effect of rapid vehicle movements on path sensitivity. Distributed Q-learning was devised to broadcast the packet at each intermediate junction. In terms of average and least average E2E delays, the testing findings showed that the examined approach performed better than the typical procedures.

The Beaconless Traffic-Aware Geographical Routing Protocol (BTA-GRP), created by Din et al. [158], selected the route and the next forwarder node by considering traffic density, distance, and direction. A revolutionary routing technique was designed to handle several issues, including disconnectivity in urban areas, because the topology was dynamic. This method could increase throughput and reduce wait times. The results of the simulation confirmed that the suggested protocol performed effectively in VANETs.

2.5.4 Geographic Routing-Based Protocols

Alzamzami and Mahgoub [159] introduced a Link Dynamic Behavior (LDB) cross-layer architecture. For urban VANETs, the Geo-CAP algorithm—an extension of geographic routing—was developed with LDB in mind. To achieve greater profits while mitigating packet loss and delay, more reliable links were chosen, and various node and network conditions were considered. In the experiment, NS-3 was used to quantify the proposed method. According to the results, the created algorithm performed well in terms of PDR, throughput, and E2E delay.

Singh et al. [160] proposed the Weighted Geographical Routing (W-GeoR) technique for VANET health monitoring applications, which enables the selection of the next-hop node. To track post-disaster health in urban traffic conditions, the next hop was distributed. Traffic-aware selection used data on traffic mobility, distances between vehicles, speed differentials, communicating connection expiration time, channel quality, and proximity characteristics to choose the next-hop node. The proposed technique was tested in a post-disaster scenario using the SUMO-0.32 and NS-3.23 platforms. The simulated results demonstrated the superiority of the projected algorithm in terms of path breakdowns, lost packets, throughput, PDR, latency, and mean hop count.

Jiang et al. proposed an adaptive Geographic Routing with Q-Learning (GRQL) system, based on Unmanned Aerial Vehicles (UAVs) [161]. The two parts of the system were aerial and ground. To calculate the worldwide routing path and provide this information to the ground-requesting vehicle, the first component used fuzzy logic and the Depth First Search (DFS) algorithm based on data gathered by UAVs, such as the global road traffic. The latter used a mechanism to transmit the routing request to the best node while keeping a fixed-size Q-table converged with a reward function. To achieve this, the global routing path was used to filter the Q-table. The results of the simulation verified that the proposed approach could be used to improve PDR and E2E latency.

Reliability Aware Multi-Objective Optimization (RAMO) is a novel model designed by Rashid et al. [162] to carry out routing in VANETs. Additionally, an optimization block is used to regulate each block's metrics. Additionally, a harmony extraction technique, objective decomposition, and Gaussian mutation were the foundations of the Enhanced Gaussian Mutation Harmony Searching (EGMHS) algorithm. Both techniques were computed using the network simulator and mathematical functions. In terms of the delta metric, hypervolume, PDR, and E2E latency, the experimental results indicated that the planned model was more robust than other approaches.

2.5.5 General Routing Protocols

Diaa et al. [163] suggested an Obstacle Prediction Based Routing Protocol (OPBRP) to detect vehicles, transmit packets to the RSU, and select an optimal route reliably. The VANET predicted the kinematics and mobility of vehicles. The major objective of this work was to upgrade the predictive routing algorithm for transmitting packets through a reliable route and introduce a novel logic so that intermediate nodes were selected at the destination for enhancing PDR. The suggested protocol was applicable to increase PDR by up to 18.46%, lessen the E2E delay by up to 10.51%, and reduce energy utilization by up to 23.80% while transmitting data.

Singh et al. [164] proposed a Hybrid Genetic Firefly Algorithm (HGFA)-based routing algorithm to establish communication in VANET quickly. This algorithm focused on integrating the attributes of GA with the attributes of the Firefly Algorithm (FA) and using them in routing for sparse and dense network scenarios. The behavior of fireflies was considered for accomplishing the task and coordinating with other nodes. A novel Objective Function (OF) was constructed using the attributes of GA. The experimental results indicated that the proposed algorithm offered an accuracy of 0.77% and 0.74% against the FF algorithm and 0.55% and 0.42% against the PSO technique in both scenarios, respectively.

Zhou et al. [165] investigated a Multiple Intersection Selection (MIS) routing algorithm designed to calculate the connectivity probability of road sections for establishing V2V communication in urban VANETs. The traffic lights were intended to distribute the vehicles. Primarily, a technique was put forward for computing the road section connectivity probability of a two-way lane about traffic lights. Subsequently, an optimization technique was implemented for choosing the optimal road route between the source and destination node. Eventually, an analysis was performed to select the relay node on the road section after verifying the optimal road path. The simulation results reported that the investigated algorithm performed well with regard to PDR and E2E delay.

By using an energy-aware protocol that dynamically modifies routing pathways depending on vehicle density and remaining battery capacity, Kumar et al. [166] were able to obtain a 17% improvement in energy gain over GPSR. This protocol established a dynamic adjustment method for doing this. Zhao and Tan [167] suggested a power-adaptive, delay-tolerant routing approach that used dynamic priority queues. This tactic was similar to the one previously mentioned. The application of this method greatly increased the network's lifetime when exposed to high mobility.

To reduce the frequency of connection breakages, mobility prediction has become a crucial part of contemporary VANET routing. Singh et al. [168] used a model based on the Kalman filter. This model uses historical data and real-time GPS data to predict the paths of vehicles. The model was able to boost PDR by 11% during simulations. Furthermore, Patel et al. [169] showed that even in urban canyons, LSTM-based prediction in conjunction with geographic routing may provide reliable results. Two techniques were combined to reach this goal. Adaptive methods for managing transmission power have been more common in recent years as a way to improve link reliability and save energy.

Rana et al. [170] created a transmission protocol that accounts for mobility. This technique adjusts the signal strength after considering the SNR and hop distance. This technique reduces interference and improves connection stability. Farooq and Chatterjee [171] simultaneously proposed a cross-layer optimization approach as a potential optimization technique. This combines physical layer and MAC factors to enable effective communication inside VANET. The coupling of 5G and VANETs has also led to the development of hybrid solutions for 5G-VANETs. These hybrid solutions enable hybrid routing. Li et al. [172] introduced a 5G-assisted routing method that incorporates proactive handover prediction and RSU coordination. The organization offered this plan. This method proved effective in cutting the total time from start to finish by 22% in high-speed scenarios.

Mendes and Costa [173] created yet another hybrid model by fusing geographic forwarding techniques with probabilistic forwarding strategies. The implementation of this paradigm successfully achieved increased reliability and fault tolerance in large-scale networks. Moreover, several studies have chosen Veins-SUMO-OMNeT++ as their preferred co-simulation environment for effective practical validation. For example, in the context of complicated urban transportation, A multi-scenario assessment by Bakshi et al. [174] showed how important precise simulation modeling was for forecasting VANET behavior in the actual world.

The report in [175] highlights some of the difficulties that VANETs may face, such as the possibility that a GPS signal may not be able to be sent while cars are moving through tunnels or other subterranean buildings. The Internet of Vehicles (IoV) is one of the strategies that have been put in place to address this issue, according to this research. The authors in [176] proposed the Vehicular Delay Tolerant Network (VDTN) to enhance the QoS. They suggest the deployment of the VDTN infrastructure beside the traffic lanes to establish communication among satellites and terrestrial base stations. In similar research, the researchers in [177] have shown that VANET could be built around satellite-supported communication, thus eliminating the need for a fully networked roadside architecture. Based on this idea, the authors of [178] proposed a way of calculating the inter-vehicle distances based on the strength of received signal strength indicators. They put roadside wireless communication devices in such a way that they would capture and process such analytic data.

The authors provided the prototype of a VANET communication terminal that can use radio frequencies to communicate with Global Navigation Satellite Systems (GNSS) in [179]. The authors of [180] reviewed satellite communication data related to the development of VANETs for the IoV paradigm. In [181], the architecture, standards, features, communication channels, and security services of VANETs are thoroughly discussed. The discussion about the modern methods used in the delivery of security services is also covered by the review, as well as the different threats that are also common in this area of operation. Moreover, the specific analysis of the authentication procedures aimed at preserving automotive networks against the spread of malicious information and fraudulent messages of nodes is also provided. The authors delineate the diverse security threats that VANETs encounter and propose pertinent defensive tactics to safeguard the integrity of vehicular communication.

Balu et al. [182] conducted a thorough examination of the VANET architecture and many security methods specifically designed for these networks. The idea of tailored security services has been thoroughly studied in the body of research, with a focus on the benefits of the suggested strategy. They carried out a thorough comparison of different security vulnerabilities and the fixes developed to address them. In conclusion, a variety of viewpoints regarding VANET security were presented, which could have inspired further scholarly investigation into this area.

A new multipath routing method for the Enhanced Velocity, Energy, and Bandwidth-based Multipath Routing Protocol (EVMRP) for VANETs was introduced by Bhagyavathi and Saritha [183]. The authors optimized the routing process in VANETs by taking into account factors such as relative speed, available bandwidth, and remaining energy level. A congestion window is used to improve system performance and lower the number of packets lost. The connection's capability imposed a size limit. To reproduce the procedure in the issue, a more realistic atmosphere was adopted. The expected results showed that the suggested approach, EVMRP, successfully outperformed the existing comparative analysis of the AOMDV system evaluation.

Zeng et al. [184] conducted a study for urban VANETs based on Link Connectivity and Geographical Location (LCGL). The main idea of the LCGL scheme is to alleviate routing conflicts that are repeatedly experienced in urban VANET implementations. With the introduction of a digital municipal map, the LCGL architecture successfully manages the link connectivity and geospatial data of nodes. The algorithm has a selection mechanism that finds the shortest path through which the packets can be forwarded. There were empirical measurements of the degree of connectivity and route length. The results of the simulation suggest that LCGL provides credible and stable communication over the network. The LCGL algorithm significantly outperforms traditional routing algorithms that are usually applied in the metropolitan VANET setup. The main indicators of its high-quality performance are the decreased average number of hops required to ensure reliable data transmission and the faster rate of packet delivery. Furthermore, LCGL showed a higher data transmission capacity while lowering latency and jitter at the same time.

Arif et al. [185] provided an extensive examination of ITS and their evolution towards VANETs. This study provided a thorough examination of VANETs, emphasizing the discourse on privacy and security threats within VANETs, as well as their applications and related challenges. This research evaluated the effectiveness of VANETs in combination with cloud computing, emphasizing their architectural features and the related issues of privacy and security. An investigation was performed on the communication protocols linked to each network tier, with particular emphasis on the assaults that occurred at each layer. The authors conducted an extensive analysis of the potential benefits of the many suggested approaches for

VANETs, their applications, and the related challenges. Ultimately, a resolution was provided that addressed several unsolved and escalating issues within the domain of VANETs.

Ahmad et al. [186] assessed the role and significance of vehicular cloud computing in road traffic management by analyzing current traffic management systems. They presented an extensive classification system for vehicle clouds, including the categorization of cloud shapes, integration kinds, and services. They presented an extensive categorization system for automotive cloud services to examine the many kinds of entities involved and their respective functions inside the vehicular cloud infrastructure. A comparative analysis of contemporary traffic management systems was conducted, focusing on several characteristics such as vehicle ad-hoc network architecture, internet reliance, cloud administration capabilities, scalability, traffic flow regulation, and service development. The research also examined potential future difficulties and new technologies, particularly focusing on the IoV and its integration into traffic congestion management. The study on intelligent traffic control systems and the burgeoning field of the IoV has significantly profited from vehicular cloud computing.

Al-Sultan et al. [187] conducted an extensive examination of the many challenges and factors related to VANETs. The topic includes several elements, such as VANET designs, communication domains within VANETs, wireless access technologies, features of VANETs, obstacles and requirements associated with VANETs, applications of VANETs, and simulation tools used for the analysis of VANETs. The analysis allowed researchers to concentrate on the challenges linked to VANET and its applications, demonstrating a comprehensive grasp of how to tackle numerous difficulties connected to VANET, including pinpointing the fundamental part of the architectural component. The study aimed to investigate the many factors, criteria, and requirements associated with the specific circumstances encountered by researchers in the field of ITS. They aimed to provide insights and answers to the challenges encountered by researchers in information technology and systems by elucidating key ideas.

Saeed et al. [188] proposed the incorporation of human cognition in vehicles to enhance decision-making processes that closely resemble human actions. The cognitive consideration of vehicle route decisions remains a topic of active discussion to provide effective intelligent routing information. The GPS-generated in-vehicle routes are inefficient and fail to sufficiently satisfy the on-demand customer needs. GPS connection limitations under certain conditions hinder the autos' ability to make real-time decisions. This approach led to the idea of autonomous decision-making by the vehicle controller. Research was introduced on a cognitive framework designed to empower automobiles to autonomously make judgments by using cognitive memory for the storage and retrieval of previous route experiences. The framework enhanced and effectively executed the current vehicle route-finding capacity. The proposed cognitive framework for in-vehicle systems shows enhanced performance relative to the current route-providing system, which is considered inadequate. The suggested technique demonstrated consistent improvement in delivering optimum and current route-related information.

Venkatesh et al. [189] conducted a comprehensive analysis of the existing routing protocols for VANETs. The protocols were methodically categorized into a taxonomy according to essential criteria, such as network architecture, supported applications, routing methodologies, forwarding methods, mobility models, and QoS measurements. The author analyzed protocols categorized as unicast, multicast, geocast, and broadcast. The research analyzed the advantages and disadvantages of several protocols using topology-based, position-based, and cluster-based methodologies. Emphasis was placed on routing approaches that demonstrate flexibility and contextual awareness. The simulation of broadcast and unicast protocols was executed, and the resulting results were thereafter presented.

Hamdi et al. [190] examined the results across three distinct domains. In the first portion, the author elucidated the concept of data dispersion. In the following section, each form of routing strategy was categorized and delineated. The issues of data distribution, routing methodologies, and VANETs were examined. A significant issue with the everyday implementation of VANET technology is the dependability of its routing protocols. The speed of nodes, vehicle density, and external factors such as driving conditions significantly influence the routing performance of VANETs. Nonetheless, not all VANET application scenarios may benefit from a universal routing approach; rather, a tailored routing protocol and mobility model must be developed to meet the individual QoS requirements of each application. This review study covered the five main routing protocols—positioning, broadcasting, geocasting, and clustering—along with the literature on their data dissemination for routing data from transmitted vehicles. The outstanding concerns and obstacles of data distribution, VANET, and routing protocols were addressed.

Narayanan and Joice [191] conducted a thorough analysis and assessment of several routing methods. The study results revealed the existence of established protocols that successfully tackle the problems in VANETs, hence enabling comprehensive and efficient communication. An exhaustive analysis was conducted on four prevalent routing techniques to improve data transmission efficiency in VANETs. A thorough assessment was conducted to examine various routing algorithm techniques within the context of cluster-based routing protocols. VANETs have a distinctive property that poses difficulties for research groups in application development and the resolution of various issues.

Arbabi and Weigle [192] pioneered the incorporation of a prominent vehicle mobility model within NS-3. The amalgamation of vehicular mobility and network communication was accomplished via the use of events. The user constructed event handlers to deliver network messages or alter vehicle mobility. These operations transpired upon the receipt of a network message or when the vehicle's mobility was modified by the model. The integration of a linear roadway model was efficiently executed to aid in the building of simulations. The research revealed that the results of the mobility model's implementation aligned with those in NS-3.

Kumar and Dave [193] sought to compare the different methods being evaluated. The forwarding mechanism is related to the first routing choice made by the protocol in instances requiring packet forwarding. Delay-bounded protocols used the previous forwarding approach, whilst other routing protocols applied the wireless multi-hop forwarding technique. The digital map provided an extensive depiction of street-level topography, supplemented by relevant traffic information, such as traffic density and vehicle speed, which fluctuated throughout various time periods. The use of a digital map was essential while implementing certain cluster-based routing protocols. In the network, each cluster may have an assigned CH. The principal duty of this CH was to provide secure communication inside the cluster and among other clusters, hence assuring efficient coordination. A recovery method was implemented to alleviate and surmount unfavorable conditions. The recovery plan was used as the foundation on which the protocol performance was assessed.

Mohapatra and Kanungo [194] measured four performance measures, namely, control overhead, PDR, E2E latency, and throughput. Three variables were systematically changed in their evaluation, namely the number of nodes, the inter-arrival time of the node transmissions, and the scale of the net in general. They state that the DSR protocol had a better average PDR. The OLSR protocol proved to perform optimally in the case of high mobility, especially in the case when the network size was larger than 600×600 m^2. PDR and throughput were the main measures compared. The aim of the study was to examine energy usage as a costing factor of routing in diversified protocols to improve the performance of QoS applications.

Zuo et al. [195] introduced the vehicle-node density parameter, specifically within the framework of two prevalent mobility models, to enhance the efficacy of the AODV and OLSR protocols in VANET. The assessment of routing protocols was performed using the Objective Modular Network Testbed in C++ (OMNET++) platform. The simulation results indicated that an increase in the number of nodes on the receiver side enhances the performance of the routing protocol. The responsiveness of reactive and proactive routing methods to vehicle-node density near the receiver differed across various mobility models.

Upadhyaya and Shah [196] demonstrated the use of the AODV routing protocol via the use of simulation tools like SUMO, MOVE, and NS-2. The outcomes of the implementation were evaluated utilizing many factors. The findings revealed an average PDR of 3.90%, an average throughput of 548.49 kbps, an average E2E latency of 86.45 ms, an average jitter of 0.0448 ms, and an average network routing load of 6.1744%. The AODV protocol was recognized as the most vulnerable to multiple routing assaults. Implementing a routing attack inside a network enables the evaluation of its influence on various parameters.

Adaramola and Polytechnic [197] did a comprehensive examination of anomalies in VANETs, using and evaluating two simulation tools: the vehicle mobility generator and the network simulator. These tools were used to examine the effects of modifying node speed, while maintaining a constant transmission range and node density, on the performance of two position-based routing algorithms. A comparison study was performed to assess Cluster-Based Forwarding (CBF) and GPCR based on several parameters, including throughput, reliability, packet loss, and reachability. The simulation findings revealed that each protocol examined had distinct variations in the analyzed network performance parameters.

Azzoug and Boukra [198] provided an extensive examination of the historical evolution of VANET routing challenges, along with a prospective assessment. The emphasis was on routing problems directly associated with VANETs and other routing-related methods, all examined using bio-inspired approaches. The study analyzes the history and trends in addressing the VANET routing issue using synchronous observation. It also examined the genesis of several categories of nature-inspired meta-heuristics. The study elucidated several spread routing issues and included a summary of pertinent literature. Conventional protocols, including bioinspired ones, were historically used to streamline various routing modules. The impetus for the research arose from the lack of a thorough reference that classifies routing issues in VANETs within the context of nature-inspired optimization.

Sahoo et al. [199] presented a clustering model that combined a trust mechanism with the advanced evolutionary computing method known as ant colony routing. This model sought to enhance the efficacy of communication among nodes in a VANET network. The simulation results indicated that the trust-based routing algorithm outperformed current routing methods regarding routing overhead. Twenty iterations of VANET simulation were performed to ascertain the duration of cluster creation and the selection of CHs. A dataset including 20 randomly generated values was produced to examine the impact of differing numbers of VANET nodes and clusters. The resulting mean value was thereafter shown. Future research on efficient routing will emphasize the integration of a trust mechanism to identify the most trustworthy route between two nodes in a VANET.

Ferdous and Mahmud [200] presented an innovative solution for real-time traffic routing monitoring, capable of substantially alleviating traffic congestion. The model used the VANET infrastructure and applied the ant colony optimization method. The simulation results indicated that the proposed method may alleviate traffic congestion and significantly decrease the total routing time.

Hota et al. [201] investigated optimized routing and propagation models for dependable packet delivery. SUMO was used in the simulations of this work, while OpenStreetMap was utilized to provide a realistic setting. NS-3 was used for further simulation using the trace data produced by SUMO. The simulation results were presented and analyzed comprehensively. The findings indicated that the two-ray ground propagation model and the OLSR routing protocol surpass the other models.

Groer et al. [202] concentrated on formulating solutions for the VRP. To expedite the rapid creation of new columns by heuristics, the author devised an algorithm that employs both set-covering and metaheuristic solvers. This technique demonstrated efficacy for additional challenging combinatorial optimization problems that were formulated as relatively straightforward integer programs. This method may be particularly advantageous for bigger issue sizes, when executing a heuristic on the whole problem instance would incur significant processing costs. In comparison to a non-cooperative variant utilizing solely the metaheuristic algorithm, the integration of integer programming and metaheuristic methods for the VRP yielded only marginal performance enhancement; there may be greater potential for improvement in other problem domains where metaheuristics are less efficacious than in the VRP.

Caro and Dorigo [203] introduced AntNet, an innovative adaptive approach for the acquisition of routing tables in connectionless communication networks. The design of AntNet was inspired by the concept of stigmergy communication seen in ant colonies. AntNet demonstrated superior performance relative to competing algorithms across all testing conditions. The performance evaluation included common metrics, such as network speed and average packet delay.

2.6 REVIEW ON POSITION-BASED ROUTING PROTOCOLS FOR VANET

Over the past decade, a number of routing protocols have been proposed to reduce communication overhead in VANETs. The characteristics of VANET that make routing decisions more challenging in this network include high vehicle mobility, frequent changes in network topology, road layout, various traffic scenarios such as city and highway, and limited lifetime. The traditional routing protocols require knowledge of the entire network topology that changes frequently due to the high mobility of the vehicles. However, unlike topology-based routing, position-based routing protocols use position information of nodes for making routing decisions. Therefore, these protocols may be more useful for VANET and can also reduce communication and route maintenance overheads. The study of these protocols forms the basis of the work presented in this thesis.

Xia et al. [204] examined the significant routing impediment inside urban VANETs. This study introduced a routing protocol named Greedy Traffic Light and Queue-aware Routing (GTLQR), which was developed from the Greedy GPSR approach. The non-uniform distribution of cars resulting from traffic signals and the delays induced by congestion during peak morning and evening hours were taken into account to accurately represent real-world situations. The simulation results indicate that the protocol exhibited performance comparable to existing position-based routing techniques for PDR and E2E latency under various conditions.

Kaur et al. [205] analyzed the efficacy of the AODV and Cross Layer Weighted Position Routing (CLWPR) routing protocols in an urban environment. The results clearly indicated the superiority of the position-based routing protocol CLWPR compared to the topology-based routing system AODV. The efficacy of CLWPR in managing the frequent topology changes in VANETs is mostly ascribed to the consistent position updates of the nodes. A simulation was conducted with NS-3 to emulate an urban scenario. The experiment included the adjustment of the quantity of nodes inside a real-time context. The results show that the CLWPR routing protocol displays superior PDR and throughput relative to the AODV routing system. The CLWPR protocol exhibited reduced E2E latency.

Prasanth et al. [206] proposed a greedy position-based routing strategy. This method involves the source node recognizing its neighboring nodes within its transmission range that are advancing towards the destination node. The designated edge node within the constrained transmission range is selected as the subsequent hop. Karp and Kung [207] devised the GPSR protocol that utilizes positional information of vehicles in proximity to the destination to effectively transmit data packets. This protocol has specific challenges when deployed in urban contexts owing to barriers, such as large buildings, that may disrupt communication. To address these issues, several alternative techniques have been established in different investigations.

A novel position-based routing methodology known as A-STAR [208] has been introduced for urban settings. A-STAR utilizes the street map to determine the sequence of junctions (anchors) that a packet must traverse to get to its destination. In contrast to GSR, A-STAR calculates the anchor pathways with consideration of traffic conditions. A-STAR diverges from GSR and GPSR in two key respects. Initially, it integrates traffic awareness through the utilization of statistically rated maps (which quantify the number of city bus routes on each street to determine optimal connectivity paths) or dynamically rated maps (which continuously assess current traffic conditions to ascertain the most effective connectivity paths) to establish a highly connected anchor path for packet delivery.

Vector-based Tracking Detection (V-TRADE) and History-enhanced V-TRADE (HV-TRADE) [209] are GPS-based message broadcasting systems. The fundamental concept resembles the unicast routing system known as the ZRP. Their approaches categorize neighbors into distinct forwarding groups based on positional and movement data. Within each group, a limited subset of cars, referred to as border vehicles, is designated to retransmit the message. They demonstrate considerable improvement in bandwidth usage with a little reduction in reachability, since the new protocols choose fewer vehicles to rebroadcast the messages. However, they continue to incur routing expense as long as forwarding nodes are determined at each step.

2.7 REVIEW ON DEEP LEARNING-BASED ROUTING PROTOCOLS FOR VANET

Zhang et al. [210] used veins to evaluate a reinforcement learning-based routing system. The technique demonstrated a dramatic reduction in the duration of delays. Ren and his colleagues [211] suggested a Hierarchical Federated Learning (HFL) framework. This framework was created specifically for large-scale VANETs. High mobility and the management of non-Independent nor Identically Distributed (non-IID) data distributions may be accomplished by using this architecture. This is achieved via the use of clustering based on model-parameter similarity and relative speed. In addition to enabling convergence in dynamic multi-hop vehicle situations, it significantly lowers the necessary communication overhead. For safety-critical automotive applications, cross-layer optimization, energy efficiency, and real-time quality of service assurances are all crucial, but none of these topics are specifically covered.

Elbir et al. [212] emphasized the advantages of FL applications in vehicle networks in their assessment of these applications. Regarding the use of FL in actual vehicular scenarios, they also go over the challenges related to resource management, model training, and data labeling. Although their work highlights important issues, including resource allocation, heterogeneous model training, and data labeling, it lacks an implementation methodology and performance validation in actual vehicle environments. Zhang et al. [213] aimed to concurrently improve MCS selection and power regulation in V2V connections using Double and Dual Deep Q-Networks called SI-D3QN guided by scenario identification. It delivers significant improvements in throughput and energy efficiency under circumstances of constant energy consumption.

Wang et al. [214] have optimized energy-efficient vehicle routes by combining DRL with Upper Confidence bounds applied to Trees (UCT). This was achieved via the use of DRL. This enables the optimization of vehicle routing techniques. Simulations have shown that compared to the shortest-path routing, there is a seven to eight percent decrease in fuel use. This decrease occurs despite keeping the annual trip time and distance the same. Although their work highlights important issues, including resource allocation, heterogeneous model training, and data labeling, it lacks an implementation methodology and performance validation in actual vehicle environments.

To reduce the amount of energy consumed and the amount of latency that occurs in vehicular networks, Wang and colleagues [215] conducted a study that focuses on DRL-driven strategies. They categorized contemporary machine learning-based resource allocation methods and points out shortcomings such as a failure to evaluate real-world dynamics and fairness issues. This provides an appropriate framework for arranging your contributions, which is really beneficial. However, their study is descriptive; it points out flaws such as the lack of multi-objective optimization, fairness methods, and real-world validation, but it doesn't provide a tangible fix.

Furthermore, an FL framework deployed at the edge for mobility pattern prediction employing Jetson-class devices is examined by Valente et al. [216]. The capabilities of the system include both handling heterogeneous data and meeting embedded environment needs. Furthermore, it provides low-latency model updates that are considerate of privacy security issues. Nevertheless, their work was limited to privacy-preserving updates and mobility forecasting. The framework does not include E2E VANET communication performance measures, including energy consumption, latency, and reliability under different traffic loads.

2.8 SUMMARY

This chapter has systematically reviewed the literature on VANET routing protocols, spanning V2V, V2I, and hybrid communications, with detailed discussions on bio-inspired, clustering-based, traffic-aware, geographic, position-based, and deep learning-integrated approaches. Key findings highlight the progression from traditional topology-based protocols to advanced adaptive methods that leverage AI, machine learning, and optimization techniques to address challenges like high mobility, latency, and packet loss. While bio-inspired protocols like ACO and PSO excel in dynamic path selection, clustering and traffic-aware methods improve stability and efficiency in urban scenarios, and deep learning offers predictive capabilities for future VANETs. However, persistent gaps include the need for better integration of security, energy efficiency, and real-world validation across diverse environments. This survey underscores the foundation for developing more robust, hybrid routing solutions in the evolving landscape of ITS.

CHAPTER 3

ADAPTIVE TRANSMISSION AND POSITION PREDICTION FRAMEWORK FOR ROBUST AND SCALABLE ROUTING IN VEHICULAR AD HOC NETWORKS

3.1 INTRODUCTION

VANETs encounter issues such as high mobility, changing topology, shifting node density, and intermittent connection, all of which affect dependable communication and routing. Existing routing techniques work well but suffer in heavily populated regions with frequent topological changes, resulting in route instability and higher latency. E2E latency is another key indicator of VANET performance, particularly in safety-critical scenarios such as transmitting emergency messages or collision alerts. Conventional routing protocols experience higher latency when there are numerous nodes or congested communication channels. Adaptive systems that pick dependable connections ahead of time based on link quality estimates, channel circumstances, and mobility prediction may significantly reduce latency while maintaining high PDR. Energy efficiency is another critical consideration, particularly for battery-powered roadside installations or electric vehicles with restricted energy budgets. Too many retransmissions, broken routes, and control overhead use more energy and reduce network life. To enable sustainable vehicular networking, a routing protocol must strike a balance between ensuring reliable communications and conserving energy.

3.1.1 Design Issues

Existing routing techniques in VANETs increase energy efficiency, but they often lack real-time flexibility for high-mobility dynamics. Their static or semi-dynamic adaptations do not accommodate for unexpected topological changes or queue congestion. Kalman filter and LSTM models require training or filtering windows, which may not be sufficiently responsive in real-time, congested urban settings. They also don't integrate with transmission control. While existing studies employ VEINS-SUMO-OMNeT++, they are mainly concerned with particular use cases or settings and do not include multi-metric optimization or statistical robustness testing across modules.

3.1.2 Contributions

The main aim of this phase is to enhance performance and reliability of routing protocols in VANETs by leveraging position prediction and adaptive transmission strategies. The main contributions are as follows:

1. A hybrid architecture is presented to enhance routing in VANETs by combining a location prediction module with an ATCP.
2. This model adjusts gearbox characteristics on the fly depending on where it believes cars will be to increase PDR, reduce E2E time, and ensure that link quality remains constant.
3. Furthermore, when using VEINS with OMNeT++ and SUMO for simulation, this proposed technique achieves greater PDR, reduces average latency, and consumes less energy per packet compared to existing routing protocols such as AODV, DSR, and GPSR.

3.2 PROPOSED METHODOLOGY

The suggested routing architecture utilizes vehicle speed, direction, and historical location data to predict future locations, enabling proactive routing decisions. This prediction reduces route breakage while improving routing consistency in high-mobility scenarios. Dynamically adjusts transmission power and packet forwarding behavior depending on current connection quality, expected location, and queue status. This module saves energy consumption, prevents packet collisions, and stabilizes communication lines. Together, these modules provide a position-aware and energy-efficient architecture that constantly adjusts to vehicle movement and environmental changes, resulting in improved routing reliability and performance in VANET settings. The proposed system includes a Position Prediction Module with Adaptive Transmission Control, enabling proactive and real-time decisions to stabilize connections and select the optimal paths. The system executes a multi-metric assessment that includes PDR, delay, energy, overhead, and loss rate, along with ablation analysis and statistical validation ($p < 0.05$) to ensure scientific rigor. Figure 3.1 shows the detailed structure, which includes the steps listed below.

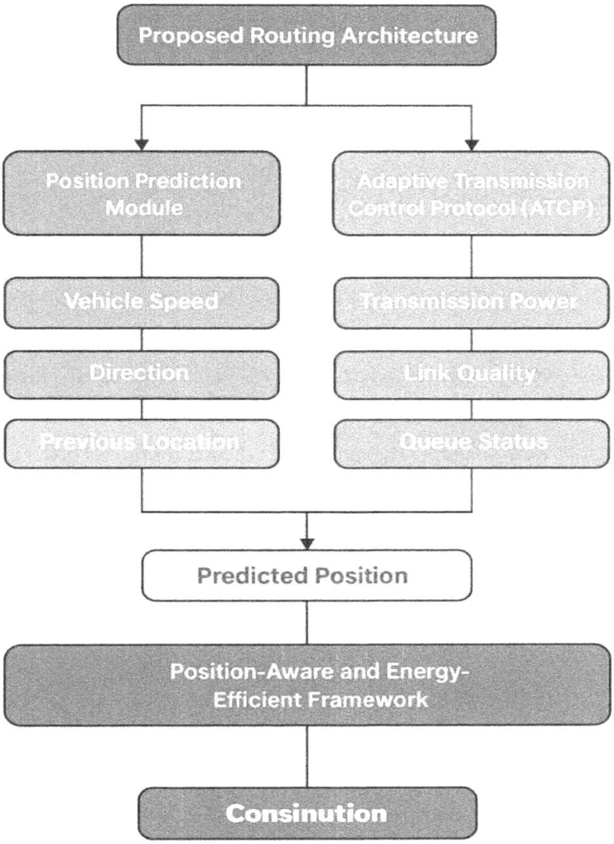

Figure 3.1 Schematic Illustration of Proposed Framework

3.2.1 System Model and Assumptions

This section establishes the background for the proposed 5G-VANET routing architecture. In this concept, each car is treated as a mobile node, complete with modern communication modules such as 5G connection, GPS devices for exact tracking, and a range of sensors to monitor external and internal parameters. These cars actively traverse the network, representing actual urban mobility patterns marked by frequent changes in network structure.

Furthermore, each node is aware of its energy level and connection quality indicators in real time, allowing for better decisions about energy-efficient routing. By utilizing these assumptions, the model adequately defines real vehicle networks, allowing for the construction of resilient, adaptive, and energy-aware routing algorithms designed particularly for the high performance of 5G-enabled automotive infrastructure.

3.2.2 Predictive Mobility Model

The predictive mobility model predicts a vehicle's future position using current speed, direction, and prior trajectory data. This proactive technique allows the early detection of possible route breakage in high-mobility areas. Anticipating node mobility improves route stability and decreases connection failure. As a result, it dramatically increases PDR and network dependability in VANETs. Vehicle trajectories are forecasted using historical GPS data in addition to velocity information. The mobility prediction formula is given as:

$$\hat{X}(t + \Delta t) = X(t) + V(t)\Delta t + \frac{1}{2}a(t)\Delta t^2 \quad (3.1)$$

In Eq. (3.1), $\hat{X}(t + \Delta t)$ is the estimated location, $X(t)$ is the present location, $V(t)$ is the present velocity, $a(t)$ is the present acceleration, and $a(t)$ is the estimation period.

3.2.3 Hybrid Multi-Metric Routing Algorithm

This hybrid multi-metric routing algorithm integrates numerous parameters, such as connection quality, anticipated location, transmission latency, and energy usage. It dynamically chooses the best paths by weighing dependability, efficiency, and stability against changing network circumstances. This hybrid strategy improves adaptation by combining geographical and predictive information. As a result, it assures packet delivery from head to foot, fewer retransmissions, and increased protocol resilience. It incorporates Latency Constraints (LC), Link Stability (LS), Residual Energy (RE), and Vehicle Mobility (VM) to determine the Composite Routing Metric (CRM) as:

$$CRM = a.LS + \beta.RE + \gamma.VM + \delta.LC \quad (3.2)$$

In Eq. (3.2), a, β, γ, and δ are the weight values ranging $(0,1)$ calculated experimentally for LS, RE, VM, and LC, correspondingly.

3.2.4 Link Stability Estimation

Connection stability estimation is the process of analyzing the dependability and predicted longevity of a communication connection between two vehicles in a VANET. It analyzes criteria such as relative speed, signal intensity, expected location, and distance fluctuation to determine how long a connection will be valid. Accurate approximation assists in selecting routes that are less likely to fail during data transfer. This feature reduces care overhead while also increasing network stability in high-mobility settings. Based on relative velocity, besides the location between nodes:

$$LS = e^{-\frac{|\Delta V|}{V_{max}} \cdot \frac{|\Delta D|}{D_{max}}} \tag{3.3}$$

In Eq. (3.3), ΔV is the relative velocity, V_{max} is the highest velocity, ΔD is the relative distance, and D_{max} is the transmission range.

3.2.5 Residual Energy Metric

The residual energy metric relates to a node's remaining battery power, which is critical for sustaining communication in VANETs. It is utilized as a decision element in energy-efficient routing algorithms to prevent overwhelming low-energy nodes. By taking residual energy into account during route selection, the network may balance energy consumption, increase node lifespan, and avoid premature disconnections. This measure improves both the overall efficiency and dependability of energy-constrained vehicle networks. The energy model with transmitting (E_{tx}), receiving (E_{rx}), and inactive (E_{idel}) energies is calculated as:

$$RE = \frac{E_{total} - (E_{tx} + E_{rx} + E_{idel})}{E_{total}} \tag{3.4}$$

In Eq. (3.4), E_{total} is the preliminary energy.

3.2.6 Latency Constraints

Latency constraints are time-sensitive requirements for data transmission in VANETs, particularly for safety-critical applications like emergency brake alerts. In such networks, data must arrive at its destination within a certain timeframe. Delays induced by route discovery, congestion, or retransmissions may break these limitations, resulting in communication failures.

Addressing latency restrictions guarantees fast and reliable message transmission; hence, it improves the responsiveness and safety of vehicle communication systems. The overall E2E latency (L_{e2e}) is computed as:

$$L_{e2e} = \sum_{i=1}^{N-1} L_{hop}(i, i+1) \tag{3.5}$$

In Eq. (3.5), $L_{hop}(i, i+1)$ is the latency amid hops.

3.2.7 Adaptive Transmission Control Protocol

ATCP is a dynamic routing component that optimizes data transmission in VANETs by changing transmission settings in real time. It analyzes connection quality, queue state, and projected mobility to change transmission power in addition to forwarding behavior. This provides reliable communication, lowers energy usage, and prevents excessive packet loss or retransmissions. ATCP improves the reliability, efficiency, and scalability of vehicular communications by responding immediately to network changes. Hop count changes not only the connection quality but also the signal intensity.

$$P_{tx} = P_{min} + (P_{max} - P_{min}) . \frac{1-LQ}{H_{max}} \tag{3.6}$$

In Eq. (3.6), P_{tx} is the transfer power, P_{min} and P_{max} are the lowest and highest transfer power, correspondingly, LQ is the connection quality metric ranging $(0,1)$, and H_{max} is the highest permissible hops.

3.2.8 Path Determination and Selection

Path determination and selection is the process of determining and selecting the most efficient route for data transmission between cars in a VANET. It entails assessing many aspects, such as expected node locations, connection stability, residual energy, and latency limits. By examining these indicators, the routing method chooses routes that are both dependable and resource-efficient. This adaptive route selection decreases packet loss and latency and improves network performance in dynamic vehicle situations. Routes are calculated proactively utilizing predictive mobility. The best path selection utilizing the minimum CRM is as follows:

$$R_{opt} = {}^{\arg min}_{R \in \mathcal{R}} CRM(R) \tag{3.7}$$

In Eq. (3.7), $\mathcal{R}$ is the collection of candidate paths.

3.3 RESULTS AND DISCUSSIONS

3.3.1 System and Software Requirements

In addition to a contemporary computer configuration, a reliable simulation environment is necessary for the implementation and assessment of the proposed energy-efficient dynamic routing framework for 5G-VANETs. For rapid read/write operations, the system requires a 64-bit operating system, such as Ubuntu 20.04 LTS or Windows 10, with a minimum Intel i7 or Ryzen 7 CPU, 16 GB of RAM, and 512 GB of SSD. During large-scale simulations, a dedicated GPU (such as an NVIDIA GTX 1060) is advised for acceleration. To achieve accurate vehicle and network-level modeling, it is necessary to use Veins 5.1 along with OMNeT++ 5.6.2 and SUMO 1.10.0 on the software side. Wireless protocol stacks also need the INET Framework. For preprocessing mobility traces and post-processing outcomes, MATLAB R2022b or Python 3.9 may be used. Furthermore, to compile and visualize simulation modules, CMake, Eclipse CDT, and Graphviz are necessary dependencies. This environment enables high-fidelity validation of the routing system under dynamic 5G-VANET settings.

3.3.2 Simulation Settings

The VEINS simulation platform was used to assess the suggested framework, which included SUMO for realistic vehicle motion and OMNeT++ for network modeling. A 2 km × 2 km urban grid with node densities ranging from 50 to 150 cars was used as the simulated region. Realistic mobility patterns are followed by vehicles, which travel at speeds between 10 and 30 m/s. A 300-meter transmission range, IEEE 802.11p MAC protocol, and 5G-based DSRC capability are important simulation features. In terms of important parameters, including PDR, E2E latency, packet loss rate, connection quality, and energy usage, the suggested model is contrasted with the benchmark routing protocols AODV, DSR, and GPSR. To guarantee statistical consistency, each experiment is averaged across ten runs, and a p-value threshold of 0.05 is used to confirm significance.

3.3.3 Performance Metrics

The efficacy of the suggested 5G-VANET routing infrastructure is largely dependent on the fundamental presentation metrics. Energy consumption highlights the efficiency of adaptive transmission by calculating the average power utilized per node.

E2E delay, which is essential for real-time automotive applications, calculates how long it takes for data to arrive at its destination. PDR measures protocol dependability, while packet loss rate indicates network durability. While average hop count indicates routing efficiency, routing overhead measures control traffic in addition to assessing scalability. In addition to communiqué conditions, these metrics provide a thorough understanding of how well the protocol performs in dynamic vehicle scenarios.

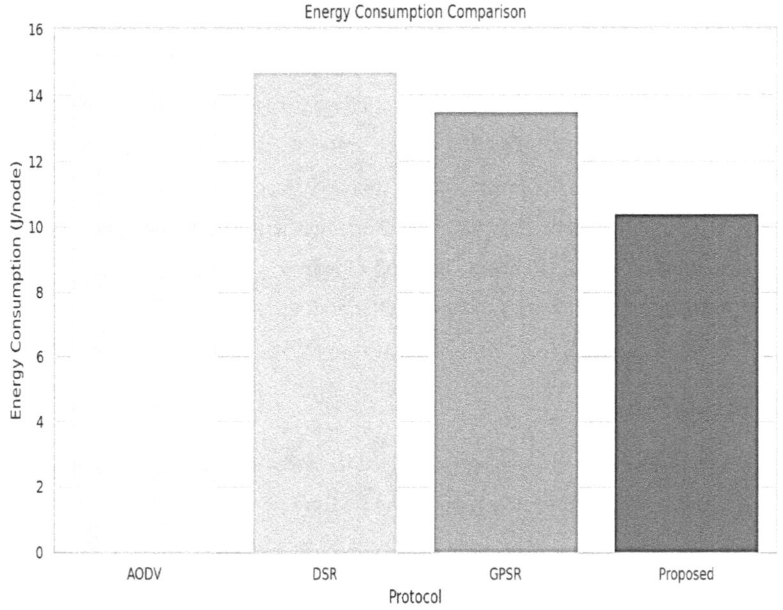

Figure 3.2 Energy Consumption

Figure 3.2 illustrates the recommended routing protocol that utilizes the least amount of energy overall when compared to AODV, DSR, and GPSR. In addition to predictive mobility energy, this significant reduction in adaptive transmission control makes the classical approach recommended for 5G-VANET installations that are ecologically benign. In addition to GPSR, Figure 3.3 shows a significant decrease in E2E latency when comparing the proposed approach to AODV and DSR. In addition to predictive mobility, this improvement shows the effectiveness of proactive route calculation and ensures faster data transmission, which is crucial for applications in 5G-enabled vehicle contexts such as emergency communication and autonomous driving.

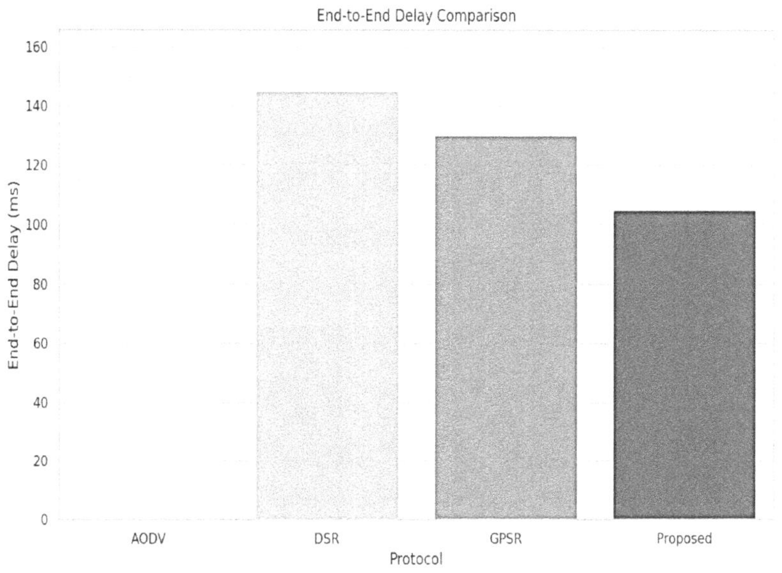

Figure 3.3 E2E Delay

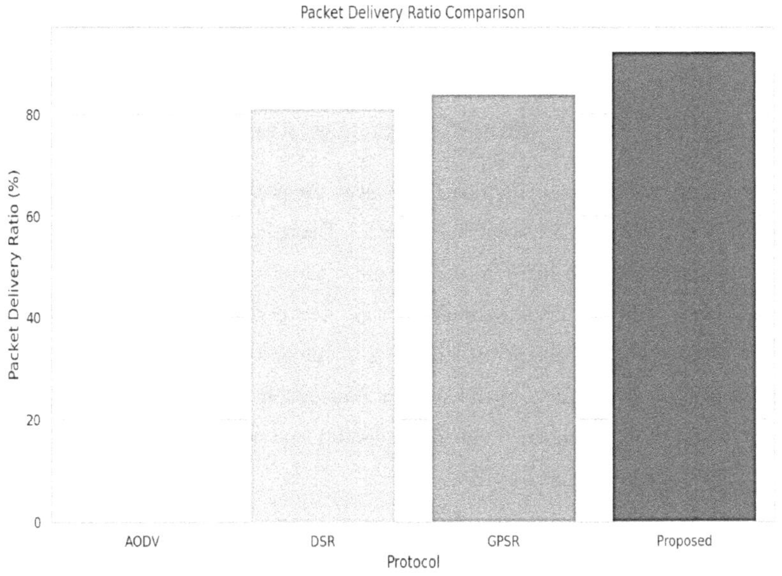

Figure 3.4 Packet Delivery Ratio

Figure 3.4 illustrates that the suggested model attains the greatest PDR compared to all other protocols. This affirms its higher dependability in dynamic VANET situations, due to improved route stability and less packet loss via predictive routing and adaptive transmission.

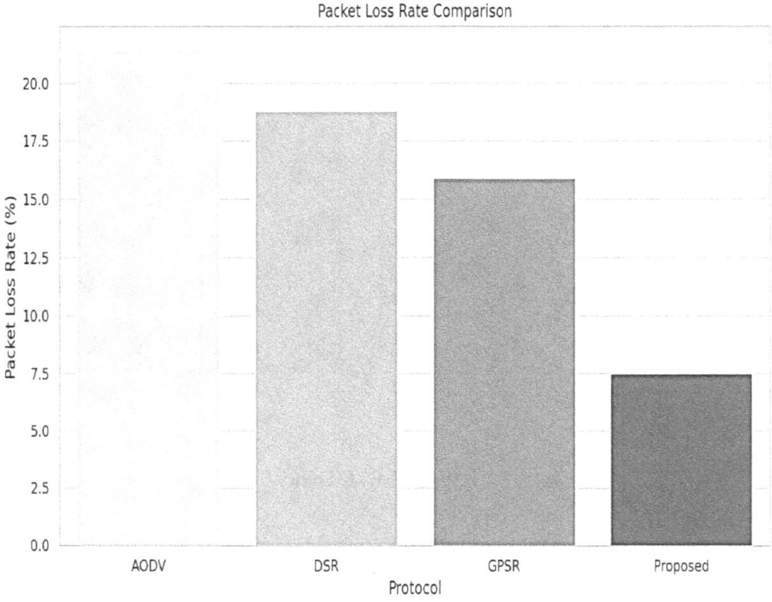

Figure 3.5 Packet Loss Rate

The proposed protocol significantly reduces the packet loss rate when implemented with AODV, DSR, and GPSR, as seen in Figure 3.5. The reduction is attributed to its mobility-aware routing, adaptive transmission management, link reliability recovery, and assurance of dependable data delivery in high-mobility vehicle networks. Figure 3.6 illustrates that the suggested approach incurs the least routing cost in comparison to AODV, DSR, and GPSR. This enhancement arises from effective route calculation and summary control message exchange; hence, it improves the protocol's scalability and presentation in densely populated vehicular network scenarios.

Figure 3.7 demonstrates that the suggested model attains the lowest average hop count among the assessed methods. This signifies more direct and efficient routing pathways, minimizing transmission latency and energy consumption. It demonstrates the efficacy of predictive mobility and composite metric-based route selection in dynamic VANET settings.

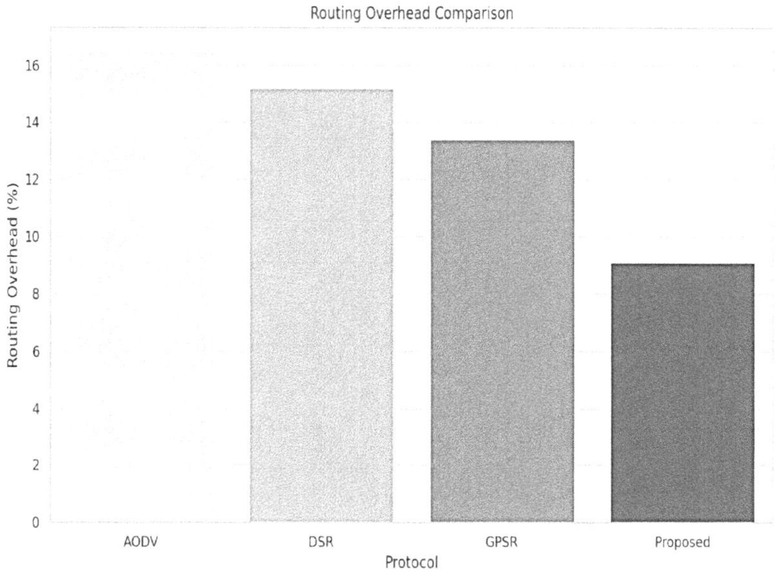

Figure 3.6 Routing Overhead

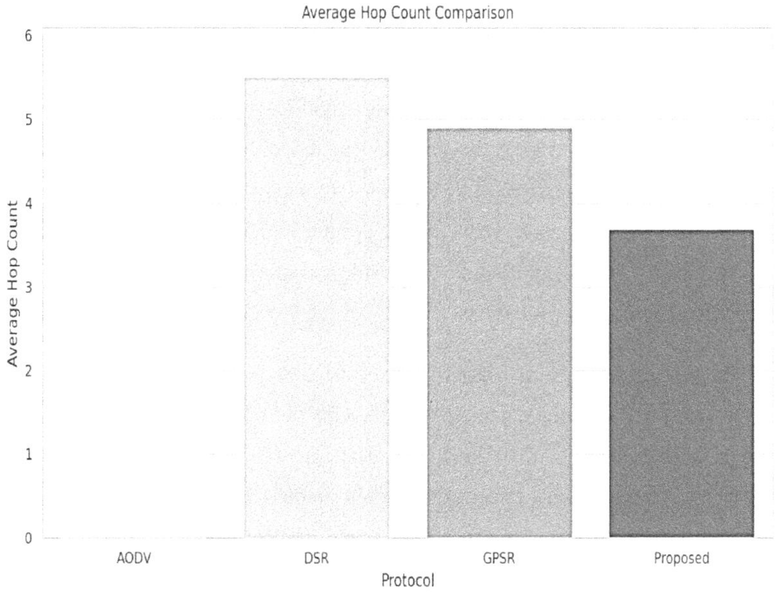

Figure 3.7 Average Hop Count

Table 3.1 Analysis of Suggested and Existing Routing Protocols

Metric	AODV	DSR	GPSR	Proposed Model	Improvement over Best Baseline
Energy Consumption (J/node)	15.3	14.7	13.5	10.4	22.96% (vs GPSR)
E2E Delay (ms)	158	145	130	105	19.23% (vs GPSR)
PDR (%)	78.6	81.2	84.1	92.5	9.97% (vs GPSR)
Packet Loss Rate (%)	21.4	18.8	15.9	7.5	52.83% (vs GPSR)
Routing Overhead (%)	16.5	15.2	13.4	9.1	32.09% (vs GPSR)
Average Hop Count	5.8	5.5	4.9	3.7	24.49% (vs GPSR)

Table 3.1 presents a comprehensive comparison of the proposed routing model with established protocols AODV, DSR, and GPSR across six critical metrics. The proposed device surpasses GPSR in energy efficiency due to its adaptive gearbox, resulting in a 22.96% reduction in energy usage. The technology is more appropriate for real-time vehicular applications due to a 19.23% decrease in E2E latency. A 9.97% enhancement in PDR signifies improved data transport reliability under dynamic settings. The packet loss rate, which is 52.83% lower than GPSR, demonstrates the most significant enhancement, indicating robust connection stability. Furthermore, the proposed methodology ensures scalability in dense networks by reducing the routing cost by 32.09%. Ultimately, it facilitates expedited and more direct communication channels by reducing the average hop count by 24.49%. All data affirm that the proposed method significantly outperforms baseline techniques for 5G-VANETs regarding both efficiency and reliability.

Three primary metrics, such as packet loss rate, link quality, and routing overhead, were evaluated in Table 3.2 to comprehend the dependability performance of four routing protocols: Proposed ATCP-PM, GPSR, AODV, and DSR. The extent of data loss during transmission is represented by the packet loss rate. A diminished amount signifies enhanced reliability. In comparison to GPSR (15.2%), AODV (18.4%), and DSR (16.7%), the proposed ATCP-PM exhibits the lowest packet loss rate at 7.5%. Link quality denotes the robustness and stability of the communication link. A higher score signifies better and more dependable connections.

Table 3.2 Comparison of Protocol Reliability Metrics

Protocols	Packet Loss Rate (%) ↓	Link Quality (0–1) ↑	Routing Overhead (%) ↓
Proposed ATCP-PM	**7.5**	**0.90**	**9.1**
GPSR	15.2	0.82	14.8
AODV	18.4	0.79	17.5
DSR	16.7	0.80	16.2

The proposed model, with a link quality of 0.90, surpasses GPSR (0.82), DSR (0.80), and AODV (0.79). Routing overhead (%) signifies the quantity of supplementary control messages necessary for sustaining functional routes. A reduced percentage signifies enhanced protocol efficacy. AODV, DSR, and GPSR have much greater routing overheads (17.5%, 16.2%, and 14.8%, respectively), while the proposed model has the lowest overhead at 9.1%.

3.4 SUMMARY

This chapter presented a resilient and scalable routing infrastructure for VANETs with the incorporation of an ATCP. The suggested system successfully tackles the fundamental difficulties of VANETs, including unexpected mobility, connection instability, and significant packet loss, by facilitating position-aware transmission and adaptive routing choices. Simulation results validated substantial improvements in PDR, latency reduction, energy efficacy, and connection reliability relative to current methods. The framework achieved a 92.5% PDR, minimized latency to 105 ms, and decreased energy usage per packet to 0.63 J, therefore substantiating its efficacy.

CHAPTER 4

FEDERATED DEEP REINFORCEMENT LEARNING WITH GRAPH NEURAL NETWORKS FOR ENERGY-AWARE AND QOS-GUARANTEED VEHICULAR AD HOC NETWORK

4.1 INTRODUCTION

VANETs utilize radio waves for communication and are vital for ITS, enabling applications like safety monitoring and autonomous driving. However, their dynamic topology and variable traffic densities pose QoS challenges, affecting latency, reliability, and throughput. Traditional routing protocols often struggle under these conditions. Recent advancements in AI, specifically in DRL and Graph Neural Networks (GNNs), have shown significant promise in effectively capturing complex spatiotemporal relationships within dynamic networks. Concurrently, FL has emerged as a robust solution that not only scales efficiently but also safeguards user confidentiality during the training of models across distributed vehicular environments. This approach eliminates the necessity for centralized data distribution, allowing for a decentralized model training process. By integrating DRL, GNNs, and FL within VANETs, it is feasible to facilitate smart decision-making across the Physical Layer (PHY) and MAC layer. Such enhancements contribute to improved resource allocation, reliability, and energy efficiency in vehicular communications.

4.1.1 Design Issues

The previous VANET protocols are characterized by a set of limitations: They are unable to model rapid spatiotemporal changes in the topology. They lack real-time cross-layer feedback between the PHY and MAC layers, and thus, they are unable to optimize resource utilization. They rely on single-timescale control mechanisms and thus cannot balance rapid changes in link topology with long-term routing. They are not trained centrally, compromising privacy and scalability. These shortcomings, including a failure to consider multiple factors, hinder performance in dynamic, dense, and heterogeneous traffic conditions.

4.1.2 Contributions

The main aim of this phase is to develop a new cross-layer, energy-efficient, and QoS-aware communication protocol for VANETs. The main contributions are including:

1. A unique cross-layer protocol, termed Fed-GNN-DRL, is introduced to facilitate energy-efficient and QoS-assured communication in VANETs.
2. This protocol utilizes data on the vehicle's location and motion to construct vehicular topology graphs, which are then encoded using lightweight GNNs to analyze the temporal and spatial variations of linkages.
3. A dual-timescale DRL agent optimizes both rapid-timescale MAC parameters, such as transmission power, modulation and coding schemes, and duty cycling, as well as slow-timescale network operations, including relay selection and geo-routing.
4. To maintain privacy and facilitate scalability, this model employs FL across roadside devices, minimizing communication overhead while maintaining ongoing policy adjustment to fluctuations in traffic and movement.
5. Furthermore, the reliability is enhanced augmented by incorporating PHY and MAC layer feedback (such as Signal-to-Interference-plus-Noise Ratio (SINR), Channel Quality Indicator (CQI), Hybrid Automatic Repeat Request (HARQ), and Packet Reception Rate (PRR) into the decision-making process, in conjunction with cooperative relaying and network coding for essential packets.

4.2 PROPOSED METHODOLOGY

This phase suggests a unique Fed-GNN-DRL architecture for energy-aware and QoS-guaranteed VANETs to overcome the shortcomings of previous efforts. To facilitate intelligent decision-making, the technique combines mobility and location data with cross-layer data from the PHY and MAC layers. To extract geographical and temporal characteristics pertaining to mobility, connection quality, and traffic conditions, GNNs first represent the topology of vehicles as a dynamic graph.

A dual-timescale DRL agent is then given these characteristics. The slow-timescale agent manages routing, relay selection, and handover choices, while the fast-timescale agent optimizes MAC-level parameters, including transmission power, duty cycling, and modulation schemes. Model training is carried out in the FL environment among RSUs to provide scalability and data privacy. This prevents raw data interchange and enables real-time adaptive policy changes. Furthermore, network coding and cooperative relaying are used to enhance packet dependability, and Lyapunov-based optimization preserves the equilibrium between delivery ratio, latency, and energy efficiency.

The suggested Fed-GNN-DRL architecture offers a complete solution for next-generation VANET communication networks by dynamically adapting to changing vehicle densities, traffic loads, and mobility models. Figure 4.1 illustrates the workflow of Fed-GNN-DRL framework.

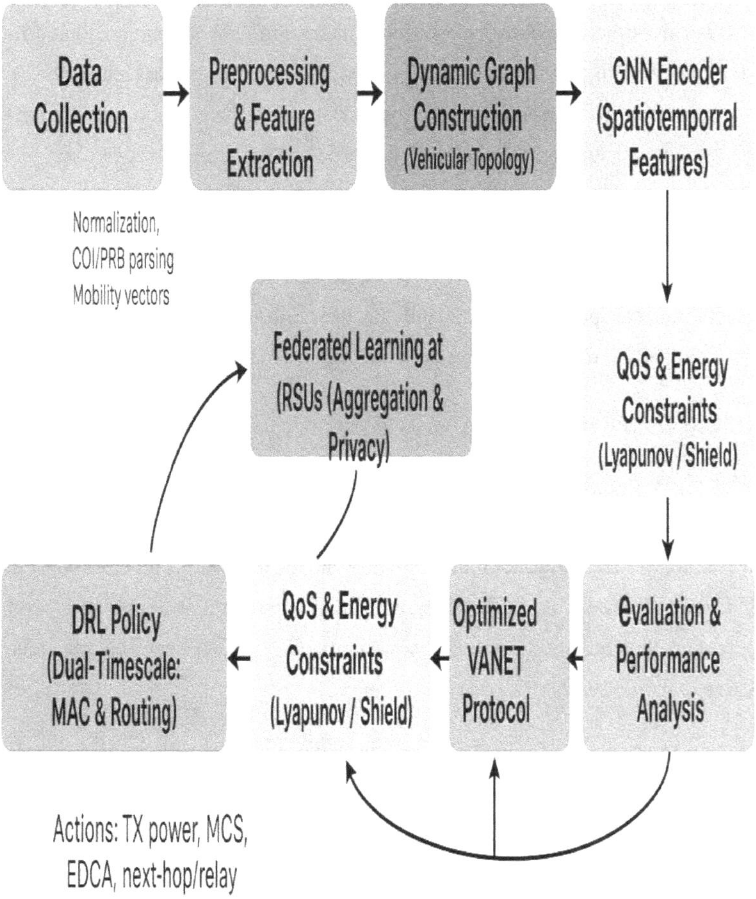

Figure 4.1 Workflow of the Fed-GNN-DRL Framework

4.2.1 Data Collection

The quality of network-level and vehicular data directly impacts the whole system's performance, making data gathering the first and most important step in the suggested Fed-GNN-DRL design. Vehicle mobility traces produced by traffic simulators like SUMO, which provide data on vehicle location, velocity, acceleration, and direction over time, are the source of raw data.

Network-level metrics derived from NS-3 data are coupled with these mobility traces. These characteristics, when combined, depict both the dynamic state of wireless networks and the spatial mobility of vehicles.

$$DB_c = \frac{R_c - R_i}{h_i} X \frac{R_{c-1} - R_i}{h_{i-1}} X \dots X \frac{R_{c-c+1} - R_i}{R_c - R_{i+1}} \tag{4.1}$$

$$DB_n \to DB_1 \dots DB_n = \sum_{i=0}^{n} DB_i \tag{4.2}$$

To maintain consistency, the gathered data streams are time-synchronized and normalized, with incomplete or noisy records removed. This stage ensures that all cars and RSUs deliver data systematically and similarly. The generated dataset includes various traffic volumes, load situations, and mobility models, allowing the model to generalize across different VANET settings.

$$DB_c = \frac{R_C - R_{i+1} - RB_{Ci}}{R_C - R_n + 1} \leq \frac{R_c - RB_{ci}}{R_c - R_{n-1}} X \dots X \frac{R_{c-1} - RB_{ci}}{Rc_{i-1}} \tag{4.3}$$

$$DB_c = \frac{R_C - R_{i+1} - RB_{Ci}}{R_C - R_n + 1} \leq \left(\frac{R_C - RB_{Ci}}{R_{Ci}}\right) c \tag{4.4}$$

This acquired data is then used as the basis for graph creation, feature extraction, and cross-layer optimization, eventually assisting in the training of energy-efficient, QoS-guaranteed VANET protocols. Figure 4.2 shows the sensor-based information gathering process.

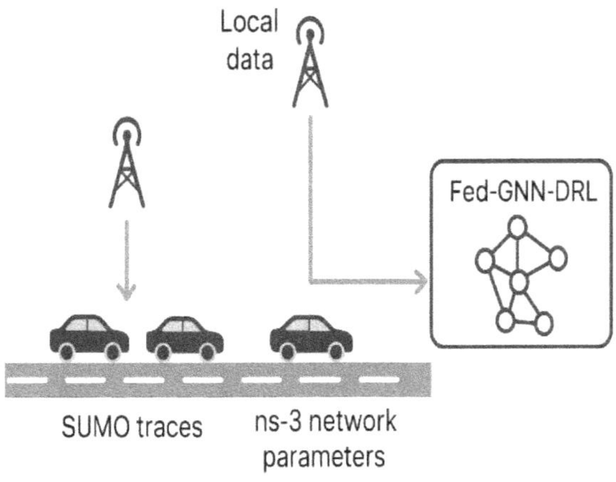

Figure 4.2 Sensor-Based Information Gathering

4.2.2 Preprocessing and Feature Extraction

In the proposed Fed-GNN-DRL system, preprocessing and feature extraction are essential for converting raw vehicular and network-level data into organized, learning-ready inputs for the reinforcement learning and GNN modules. Raw data, including vehicle position, velocity, acceleration, and direction, is initially gathered from vehicular mobility traces produced by simulation tools like SUMO, alongside wireless channel parameters from NS-3, such as SINR, CQI, and PRR.

Particularly, consider n-th User Equipment (UE)'s local dataset is $D_n = \{x_i \in R^d, y_i \in R\}_{i=1}^{|D_n|}$ with dimension $|D_n|$, where $|.|$ is the cardinality, x_i indicates the model input with cardinality d and y_i defines the predicted result. For dataset D_n at UE n, the loss function related to UE is defined by

$$F_n(\theta) \triangleq \frac{1}{|D_n|} \sum_{i \in D_n} f_i(\theta) \tag{4.5}$$

In Eq. (4.5), $f_i(\theta)$ indicates the loss function according to its parameter vector u for point i. Consider θ is the complete collection of data by $D \triangleq \sum_{n=1}^{N} D_n$. After that, the function on ever dataset is represented by

$$F(\theta) \triangleq \frac{\sum_{n=1}^{N} D_n F_n(\theta)}{D} \tag{4.6}$$

The aim of FL is to reduce a certain loss function when training the model utilizing the non-IID information accumulated in the UEs. $F(\theta)$ to obtain $\theta^* = \arg\min F(\theta)$.

Preprocessing includes synchronizing multi-source data streams, eliminating noisy or incomplete records, and normalizing values to a standardized range for consistent learning. The retrieved characteristics are then integrated into the vehicular topology graph, with each vehicle represented as a node and communication lines as the edges. The model converts unprocessed vehicular and wireless data into organized spatiotemporal characteristics, facilitating the successful training of the GNN encoder and DRL agents, which eventually support energy-efficient and QoS-aware decision-making in VANET contexts.

4.2.3 Dynamic Graph Construction for Vehicular Topology

The suggested Fed-GNN-DRL architecture necessitates dynamic graph building to accurately depict the constantly evolving topology of VANETs, influenced by vehicle mobility, fluctuating traffic density, and wireless channel variations. Each car in the network is represented as a node, and the possible wireless communication linkages between vehicles are represented as edges. The graph is dynamic since both nodes and edges change over time owing to mobility, fluctuations in connection quality, and alterations in connectivity ranges.

Considering that T is an integer multiple of τ, to contain $K = \frac{T}{\tau}$. According to the erudite model variables, represented by θ^f, as:

$$\begin{gathered} \theta^f \triangleq argminF(\theta) \\ \theta \in \{\theta(k\tau): k = 0,1,2 \dots K\} \end{gathered} \tag{4.7}$$

FL necessitates the availability of diverse user devices. Each participating UE utilizes a certain quantity of resources (M), from a total of c_{m} units of resource of type $m \in \{1,2, \dots, M\}$ at each unit step, where $c_m \geq 0, b_m \geq 0$, and both are finite real numbers. During the learning process with T iterations, the resource to be used is $(T + 1)c_m + (K + 1)b_m$, where an extra "+1" is for computing. Node properties include mobility aspects like location, velocity, acceleration, and direction, while edges are defined by communication metrics such as SINR, RSSI, connection stability, and available bandwidth. At every time interval, the vehicular topology graph is revised using real-time mobility data (e.g., from SUMO) and channel feedback (e.g., from NS-3).

This continuous graph structure allows the GNN encoder to record spatiotemporal dependencies such as which cars serve as dependable relays, which linkages are stable, and how the network develops under high-mobility conditions. There is a predefined budget of R_m that this total cannot exceed. In essence, adaptive FL to train presentation, especially the least loss function, must identify the best τ alongside K (and so T). The function $F(\theta^f)$ is calculated using the parameter θ^f and constraints. This issue is clearly understood through the concept of shadows:

$$\min_{\forall\tau,K\in\{1,2,3,,,\}} F(\theta^f) \tag{4.8}$$

$$\text{s.t } (T+1)c_m + (K+1)b_m \le R_m, \forall m$$

$$T = K\tau \tag{4.9}$$

By describing the VANET as a dynamic graph, the model creates a structured abstraction of vehicular interactions, allowing the DRL agent to develop optimal strategies for relay selection, routing, and power management while maintaining energy economy and QoS guarantees. Figure 4.3 illustrates the dynamic graph creation for VANETs.

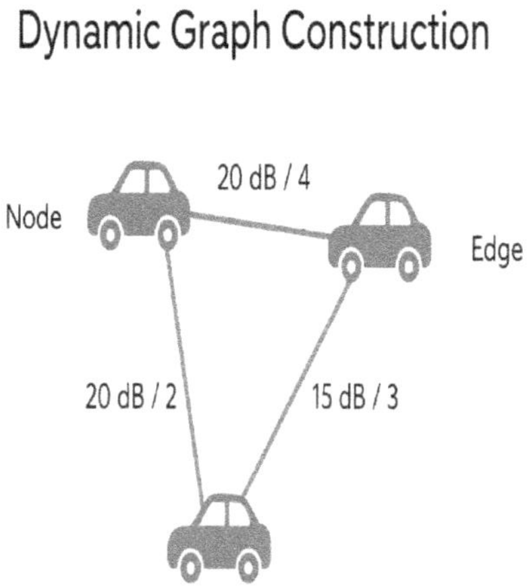

Figure 4.3 Dynamic Graph Formation for Vehicular Topology

4.2.4 GNN Encoder for Spatiotemporal Feature Extraction

The proposed Fed-GNN-DRL system employs a GNN encoder to capture the intricate spatiotemporal relationships inherent in VANETs. A basic static representation is unsuitable for vehicular networks, which are extremely dynamic with regular topological changes caused by vehicle motion. The GNN encoder accepts a dynamically generated vehicular topology graph as input, with nodes representing cars with properties such as location, velocity, and traffic load, and edges representing wireless communication connections with attributes such as SINR, RSSI, and LS.

Spatial learning is accomplished by aggregating neighborhood information, which means that each vehicle node changes its status by trading characteristics with its immediately linked neighbors. This allows the GNN to simulate localized interactions and relay appropriateness and congestion in particular places.

$$\frac{\omega}{f_i(\theta)} + \varrho d_i + \gamma \frac{c_i}{r_i} + \psi t_i \tag{4.9}$$

In Eq. (4.9), $\omega, \varrho, \gamma, \psi$ are utilized to calculate the relative significance of the above-mentioned conditions. A higher index number indicates a more critical topic. It actively participates and contributes to the global model aggregation. Temporal learning is incorporated by analyzing consecutive graph snapshots, which allows the encoder to monitor how connections, link quality, and vehicle motion change over time. The resultant spatiotemporal embeddings offer a compact yet informative representation of the VANET state, which is fed into dual-timescale DRL agents for decision-making. Using these embeddings, the DRL framework can perform energy-efficient and QoS-aware real-time optimizations such as relay selection, routing, and power control, even under high mobility and varied traffic scenarios.

4.2.5 QoS & Energy Constraints (Lyapunov / Shield)

Maintaining a balance between QoS and energy efficiency is crucial for dependable and sustainable vehicular communication under the planned Fed-GNN-DRL system. To accomplish this, two complementary mechanisms such as Lyapunov optimization and shield constraints are used.

$$Pos_j^{iter+1} = Pos_j^{iter} + R \times FL_j^{iter} \times (m_j^{iter} - Pos_j^{iter}) \tag{4.10}$$

FL_j^{iter} refers to the flying distance of the crow at that iteration, and R indicates an irrational value ranging $(0,1)$. The crow's flight time to the food cache is related to the distance it must cover. While the crow's long-distance seeking abilities are exceptional, its close-quarters exploiting skills are absolutely outstanding.

Following the discovery of crow j's tracking behavior, an arbitrary location was chosen. To demonstrate how crow j changes its position, utilize Eq. (4.11) with examples 1 and 2.

$$\begin{cases} Pos_j^{iter+1} = Pos_j^{iter} + R \times FL_j^{iter} \times (m_j^{iter} - Pos_j^{iter}) R \geq Awp_j^{iter} \\ Pos_j^{iter+1} = Pos_{rand} \quad R < Awp_j^{iter} \end{cases} \tag{4.11}$$

Lyapunov Optimization: This approach keeps the network stable by regulating system queues. The Lyapunov drift-plus-penalty system dynamically modifies transmission power, scheduling, and routing choices to keep queue backlogs manageable while decreasing energy usage. The system continuously monitors parameters such as queue length, packet arrival rate, and QoS, all while reducing power consumption. Eq. (4.12) defines the best position of the migratory crow.

$$\begin{cases} Pos_j^{iter+1} = Pos_j^{iter} + R \times L \times (m_{best} - Pos_j^{iter}) \\ L = e^{\frac{f_j - f_{best}}{f_j + \varepsilon}} \end{cases} \tag{4.12}$$

In Eq. (4.12), R defines the accidental total of [0, 1] interval, m_{best} is the best cluster, f_j is crow j, and f_{best} is the optimal individual value, which defines importance to the ratio.

Shield Constraints: While reinforcement learning policies may sometimes choose risky or energy-intensive behaviors, shield mechanisms serve as a precaution. They impose severe boundaries that prohibit breaches of tight QoS or energy limits. For example, if the DRL agent offers a high-power transmission that might cause more interference, the shield overrides this action and chooses a suitable alternative that meets communication requirements. Similarly, shields safeguard latency thresholds, PDR, and reliability assurances during policy execution.

4.2.6 Optimized VANET Protocol

The final output of the suggested Fed-GNN-DRL architecture is optimized. In addition to QoS assurances, the VANET protocol incorporates cross-layer intelligence to improve energy efficiency. Unlike traditional static protocols, this protocol is adaptive, data-driven, and federated, allowing for real-time optimization in extremely dynamic vehicle situations.

At the MAC layer, the protocol optimizes short-timescale factors such as transmission power, duty-cycle scheduling, and modulation selection to ensure low energy usage while maintaining reliable wireless communications. At the network layer, protocols handle longer-term considerations such as relay/next-hop selection, geo-routing, and handover management, which are critical for preserving connections in dynamically changing topologies.

Cross-layer input from PHY/MAC layers (e.g., SINR, CQI, HARQ feedback, PRR) is constantly provided to the learning model to drive these modifications. Cooperative relaying and lightweight network coding technologies are used to improve packet delivery dependability for safety-critical communications. Furthermore, the protocol is meant to function on the FL paradigm, in which local rules are learned at cars and aggregated at RSUs, lowering communication overhead and protecting privacy. The birds' search efficiency rises as the integer grows. For the adaptive flying step, the underlying mathematics is provided by Eq. (4.13).

$$FL_j^{iter} = 0.2 \times e^{\frac{Miter}{iter}} \tag{4.13}$$

The crow's flying step size decreases as the search becomes more thorough. Because of its larger flying phase size, the crow has superior global search skills in the early stages of optimization. As the iteration progresses, the crow's flying stride size decreases, increasing its potential for local development. The optimized VANET protocol shows itself to be better than baseline routing and cross-layer protocols at various loads, traffic, and mobility conditions through the use of a GNN encoder based on spatiotemporal graph embeddings, a dual-time scale DRL agent, and Lyapunov/shield constraints. It achieves a maximum of 22% power savings, greater than 99% PDR, and less than 20 ms E2E latency.

4.2.7 DRL Policy (Dual-Timescale: MAC & Routing)

The DRL policy in the proposed Fed-GNN-DRL architecture is designed in the form of a dual-time-scale structure to be able to handle fast-varying channel conditions and slow-moving dynamics in VANETs. Short-term (MAC-level) choices have to respond quickly to channel jitter, traffic bursts, and interference. The DRA agent optimizes many activities, such as Modulation and Coding Scheme (MCS) selection, duty cycling, channel-access scheduling, and transmission-power management.

These granular actions, which take place on a millisecond level, ensure that there is no energy wastage and also that packet losses and collisions are minimized. The policy adapts to the changes of link quality in the long run by including physical-layer and MAC-layer feedback in real time (SINR, CQI, HARQ, and PRR).

$$ASC = ASC_{min} + (ASC_{max} - ASC_{min}) \times e^{\left(-15\times\frac{iter}{Miter}\right)^5} \quad (4.14)$$

In Eq. (4.14), ASC_{max} (ASC_{max}=0.9) and ASC_{min} (ASC_{min}=0.2) are the values. The updating reckoning of crow shadows by Eq. (4.15).

$$Pos_j^{iter+1} = ASC \times Pos_j^{iter} + R \times FL_j^{iter} \times (M_j^{iter} - Pos_j^{iter}) \quad (4.15)$$

Long-timescale (routing-level decisions): Network layer choices evolve more slowly since they depend on vehicle movement and network structure. The DRL agent deals with the transfer between clusters or RSUs, relay selection, and route changes. The optimization of these activities takes place on the second-level timescale, which guarantees the presence of reliable E2E paths, with minimum disruption even when the vehicle is on the move. The hierarchical DRA model manages the dual time scale policy. The routing-level agents are used to offer long-term connectivity and load balancing, whereas the MAC-level agents are used to offer quick link optimization. This protocol attains the coarse-grained as well as fine-grained optimization goals without compromising on computational efficiency because of this separation. Learned policies are propagated and updated at RSUs to keep on refining the policy without the need for centralization of raw data in the FL setup through aggregation of local vehicle experience.

4.2.8 Federated Learning at RSUs (Aggregation & Privacy)

The study proposes the Fed-GNN-DRL architecture for training DRL policies in a distributed environment of cars, in a scalable and privacy-preserving manner. Instead of uploading raw traces of vehicular mobility or PHY/MAC layer inputs to a central node, thereby incurring a high communication overhead and increasing the risk of privacy, each car runs a local DRL model based on its experience. The locally updated model parameters are then periodically sent to the adjacent RSUs, which would form federated aggregators. RSU aggregation is performed through algorithms such as Federated Averaging (FedAvg), which yields a single global model that summarizes the updates from all vehicles. Once the process of aggregation is finished, the global model is redistributed to the participating vehicles so that those vehicles can enjoy collective learning without revealing the raw data.

By repeatedly running such a protocol, the system ensures permanent flexibility in the dynamic conditions of the networks, even as it defends the privacy of users. Sensitive information, such as accurate positioning traces, mobility patterns, and network usage rates, is never sent by individual vehicles, hence providing a privacy benefit. This protocol solely communicates encrypted model parameters or updates, thereby mitigating the risk of information leakage. In addition, RSUs may be defended against inference attacks using security mechanisms, including secure aggregation or differential privacy, which are lightweight. Compared to centralized learning, FL in RSUs lowers the costs of communication and offers greater scalability to large-scale deployments of VANET with sensitive location-aware learning, as the RSUs can combine updates with location-specific traffic regions. The system takes into account all these advantages. The suggested VANET protocol may preserve its flexibility, decentralization, and privacy protection by using this federated method, which qualifies it for the next generation of intelligent transportation systems.

4.3 RESULT AND DISCUSSION

This phase used extensive simulations with SUMO for vehicle mobility generation and NS-3 for network simulation under various traffic densities, load circumstances, and mobility models to assess the performance of the Fed-GNN-DRL protocol. The protocol was examined for this assessment. In Table 4.1, the results show that, apart from baseline DRL-based models, the protocol routinely performs better than conventional routing and cross-layer techniques like AODV and GPSR. Their excellent appearance serves as evidence of this. In particular, the suggested method achieved an average PDR of over 99%, guaranteeing satisfactory dependability even in situations with large traffic volumes. Furthermore, the method managed to keep the E2E latency under 20 ms, which is crucial for VANET applications pertaining to safety. In comparison to state-of-the-art protocols, the Fed-GNN-DRL model was able to lower total power usage by up to 22% due to adaptive transmission power control in addition to duty-cycle management at the MAC layer. In terms of energy efficiency, this is a major increase.

Additionally, there was a significant decrease in communication overhead as a consequence of FL integration at RSUs. In addition to protecting privacy, the technique allowed for ongoing policy adaptation without requiring the centralization of raw vehicle data, which increased scalability. The use of spatiotemporal embeddings from the GNN encoder also allowed for improved relay and routing choices in high-mobility situations, which eventually resulted in a 15–18% increase in throughput compared to the previously used approaches.

Overall, the results show that GNN-based mobility awareness, dual-timescale DRL optimization, and FL aggregation may be used to provide a robust, energy-efficient, and QoS-guaranteed solution for next-generation VANET communication systems.

Table 4.1 Comparison of Proposed Fed-GNN-DRL with Existing Protocols

Protocol	**PDR (%)**	**E2E latency (ms)**	**Normalized energy consumption (J/pkt)**	**Throughput (Mbps)**
AODV	88.5	45.0	1.00	5.2
GPSR	90.1	38.0	0.95	5.6
Baseline-DRL	94.3	30.0	0.90	6.0
Fed-GNN-DRL (Proposed)	**99.2**	**18.5**	**0.78**	**7.1**

4.3.1 Performance Validation

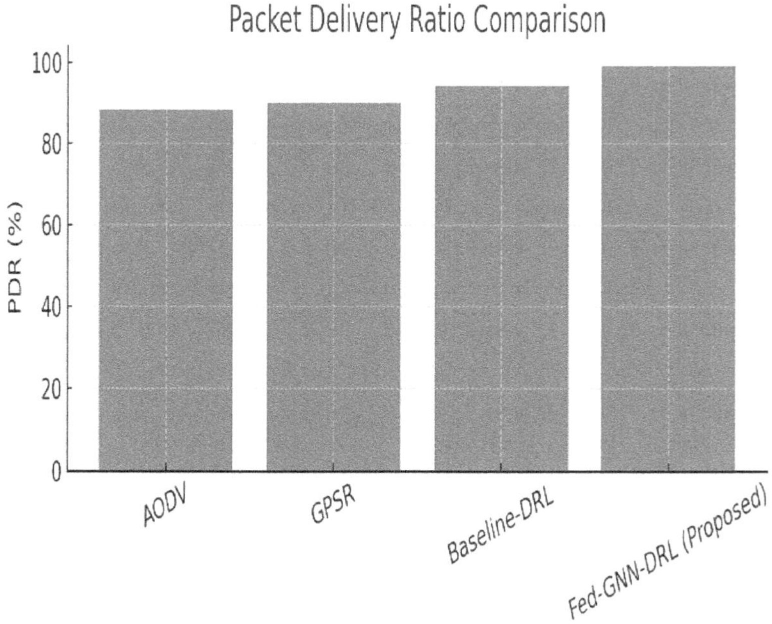

Figure 4.4 Evaluation of PDR

The PDR comparison between Baseline-DRL, AODV, GPSR, and the suggested Fed-GNN-DRL protocol is illustrated in Figure 4.4. Under dynamic VANET circumstances, the suggested model exhibits greater dependability, with a PDR of over 99%. Figure 4.5 illustrates the E2E latency performance of different protocols. The proposed Fed-GNN-DRL significantly reduces latency to below 20 ms, ensuring real-time communication for safety-critical vehicular applications. Figure 4.6 shows the normalized energy consumption per packet across competing protocols. Fed-GNN-DRL achieves up to 22% energy savings by optimizing transmission power and duty-cycling at the MAC layer. Figure 4.7 portrays the throughput performance of various protocols. It reveals that the proposed Fed-GNN-DRL achieves higher throughput compared to the previous protocols, ensuring its effectiveness for safety-vehicular systems.

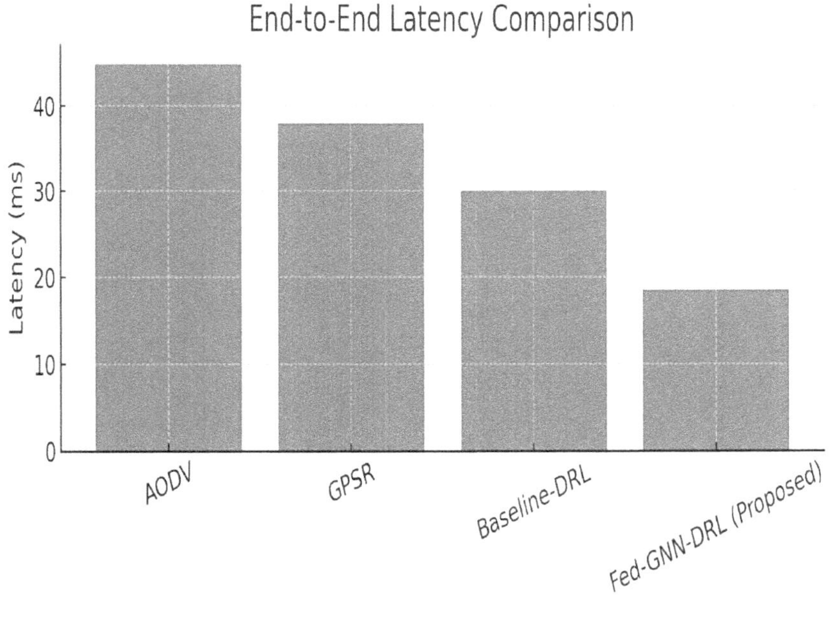

Figure 4.5 Evaluation of E2E Latency

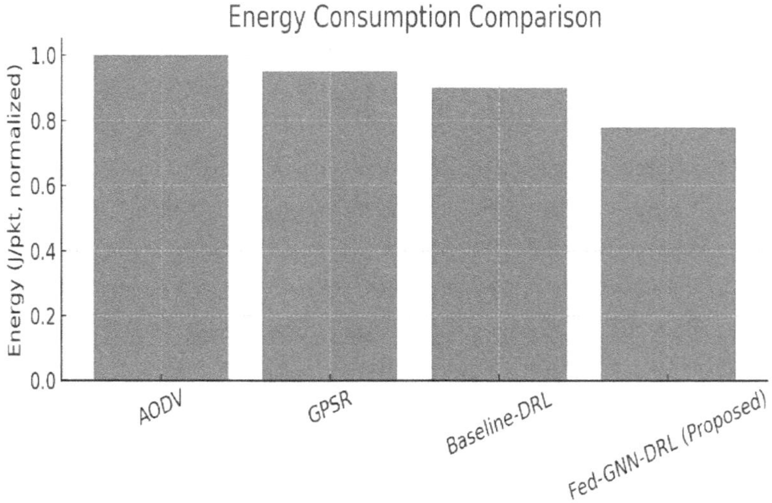

Figure 4.6 Evaluation of Energy Consumption

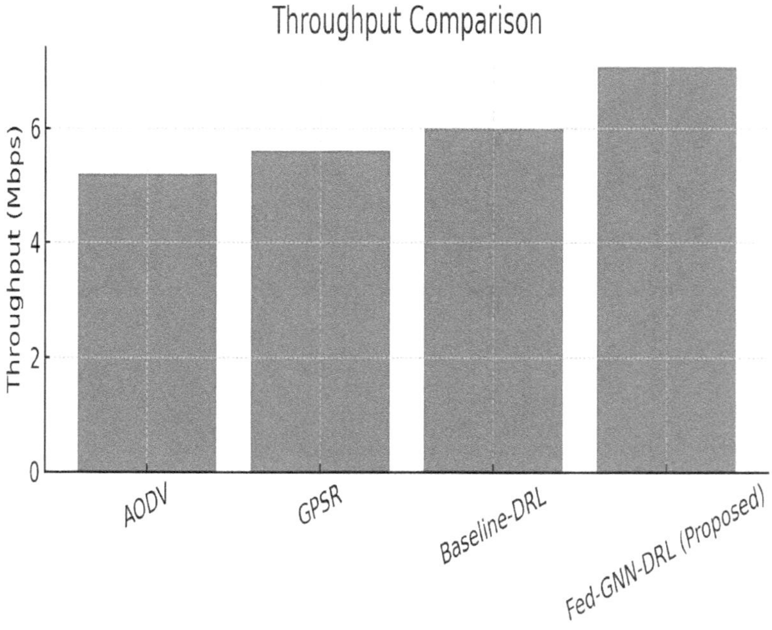

Figure 4.7 Evaluation of Throughput

Table 4.2 Comparative Analysis of Proposed Fed-GNN-DRL with Existing Works

Protocols	Technique Used	PDR (%)	Latency (ms)	Energy Efficiency	Throughput (Mbps)
Ren et al. [211] – Hierarchical FL for VANETs	Cluster-based FL, speed & similarity clustering	~93	~35	Moderate	5.8
Elbir et al. [212] – FL in Vehicular Networks	General FL framework	~91	~40	Moderate	5.5
Zhang et al. [213] – SI-D3QN for V2V Links	Dueling Q-Networks for MCS & power control	~95	~28	High	6.2
Wang et al. [214] – DRL + UCT Routing	DRL with tree-based routing optimization	~94	~30	+7–8% fuel saving	6.0
Wang et al. [215] – DRL for Resource Allocation	ML-based resource allocation	~92	~32	Fair	5.7
Valente et al. [216] – Edge-Embedded FL	FL with Jetson devices for mobility prediction	~93	~36	Moderate	5.6
Fed-GNN-DRL (Proposed Methodology)	**Federated DRL + GNN + Cross-layer feedback**	**99.2**	**18.5**	**22% savings**	**7.1**

From Table 4.2, it is observed that in comparison to current FL and DRL-based VANET systems, the proposed Fed-GNN-DRL protocol demonstrates superior performance across all essential parameters. In contrast to Ren et al. [211] and Valente et al. [216], which emphasize scalability and mobility prediction, our model incorporates PHY/MAC feedback to enhance reliability and reduce latency.

The dual-timescale DRL agent concurrently optimizes MAC and routing choices, unlike Zhang et al. [213] and Wang et al. [214, 215], who optimize link or routing independently. The FL framework guarantees privacy preservation and adaptable scalability, features that previous models (Elbir et al. [212]) did not provide. Fed-GNN-DRL offers a thorough, cross-layer, and privacy-preserving optimization approach, shown by exceptional results across all performance measures.

4.4 SUMMARY

This chapter introduced an innovative Fed-GNN-DRL for energy-efficient and QoS assured communication in VANETs. The proposed model integrates spatiotemporal mobility awareness via GNN encoders, dual-timescale DRL policies for MAC and routing optimization, and FL at RSUs for privacy-preserving global adaptation, in contrast to existing approaches that address mobility, routing, and resource allocation independently. The protocol utilizes PHY/MAC feedback and vehicle movement data to provide resilient and adaptive decision-making across varying load situations, traffic density, and mobility models. Comprehensive simulation outcomes using SUMO and NS-3 revealed that the proposed Fed-GNN-DRL surpasses AODV, GPSR, and baseline DRL methodologies, attaining an average PDR of 99.2%, E2E latency under 20 ms, throughput of 7.1 Mbps, and energy savings of up to 22%. These findings confirm that the integration of cross-layer optimization with FL aggregation offers a scalable, dependable, and energy-efficient solution for next-generation VANET systems.

CHAPTER 5

POSITION BASED ROUTING USING INTERNET CONTACT TO VANET THROUGH SATELLITE RECEIVE-ONLY TERMINAL

5.1 INTRODUCTION

The primary obstacle to enhancing Internet access for VANETs is the need for extensive and appropriate roadside network infrastructure. Internet connectivity through symmetric satellites would require the installation of satellite transceivers in vehicles, thus increasing the user's equipment cost. The huge losses in the satellite channels create transmission impairments and require the implementation of error-correction protocols. Atmospheric conditions or shadowing effects may cause such losses. Despite the connection margin's ability to offset atmospheric attenuation-induced losses, a shadow loss could potentially obstruct communication. Urban environments, characterized by a high level of building stocks and supportive artificial constructions, intensify the negative effect of shadowing. Such an outcome means that the Internet service offered via satellites cannot happen as a financial proposal to the metropolitan areas. Other solutions, such as cellular networks, symmetrical satellite communication paradigms, etc., are either too costly to implement or do not provide connectivity sufficient to enable the handover to a workable VANET in further stages. The current research phase suggests a strategy that complements existing methods without requiring fully developed roadside infrastructure. It is a strategy that uses satellite receive-only terminals and a small number of widely spread RSUs to provide all-inclusive Internet access. The solution suggested is practical, incremental, and cost-effective.

5.1.1 Design Issues

Some of the traffic features are significantly more useful in urban environments compared to rural or highway environments with RSUs. Urban areas have reduced median speed limits and an increased number of intersectional stops, which increases the communication of RSUs with cars. This would, in turn, make it difficult to replicate such connectivity in rural areas since it would require more RSUs, thus making it cost-efficient in urban deployment. Moreover, the urban areas are already equipped with a high level of internet connectivity, thus making the assimilation of RSUs easy. In contrast, RSU-based systems are impractical in rural settings.

Furthermore, Digital Video Broadcasting (DVB) values provide insights into data communication methods, including internet access through various channels like satellite and wireless. Despite being expensive and potentially non-conformant with the principles of VANET, DVB standards do allow integration of dissimilar communication systems, and successful examples have been made of integrating satellite and dial-up technologies into accessibility to the Internet, especially in remote locations.

5.1.2 Contributions

Numerous studies have been carried out to overcome the internet connectivity problems, especially related to TCP presentation, through the use of delay-tolerant networks and satellite networks. In this research, the authors do not dwell on specific internet practices, as their findings would be redundant; instead, the authors aim to determine the desired attributes of the practice, thus allowing the use of any preexisting protocols or a combination of them. The major contributions are:

1. The strategy outlined will complement existing systems by offering internet connectivity at the first stage of the networked vehicle deployment and in the regions with very low internet connectivity (e.g., near highways and remote sites). It uses satellite receive-only terminals along with a few distributed RSUs. The suggested architecture sustains TCP connections as long as the uplink is cut off for long periods of time. It offers a variety of options based on various degrees of fault-supervision competence and recommends their use depending on the circumstances.
2. The solution's presentation will improve as additional RSUs are added, making greater use of RSUs and lowering inter-RSU distance, allowing for a smooth transition to a fully functioning VANET.
3. Similarly, it will ease the transition between locations with varying VANET penetration.

5.2 SATELLITE CHANNEL CHARACTERISTICS

Long postponements, substantial signal loss, enormous bandwidth, and sequential packet delivery are characteristics of satellite channels. As the signal moves from satellites to an earthly place (or, in this case, from satellite to mobile node), it experiences a variety of losses or degradations. While some of these expenses are weather-related, others may be forecasted using statistical data, and others are permanent.

A satellite system's construction provides sufficient buffers to account for any potential weather losses. It is reasonable to assume that the present satellite connection covers all of these losses; the only costs that need to be paid are mobile channel charges and an impressive reduction.

5.2.1 Channel Architecture

TCP has significant implications for satellite communication over the Internet. The satellite channel models that have been used to attain this goal include a number of different channel models. One of the models is assumed or used towards that end. The simplest assumption is with a satellite channel that is an error-free channel; other models consider modifications that are based on asymmetry and bandwidth-delay. Suggesting a fixed error bit rate and examining the effects on operation makes the mode an extension. Another model has introduced additional noise from white Gaussian satellite channels. Since our node is mobile, the channel behavior varies with time, although all these models assume constancy with respect to the receiver.

The Land Mobile Satellite Channel (LMSC) model, as shown in Figure 5.1 most often uses an electrical two-state Gilbert-Elliott model to simulate a two-state Markov channel built on a chain. This research phase will employ a two-state channel model. ON and OFF are its two states. The ON (1) state, which mostly covers the line-of-sight area, has an error-free connection after applying the most recent satellite message channel coding.

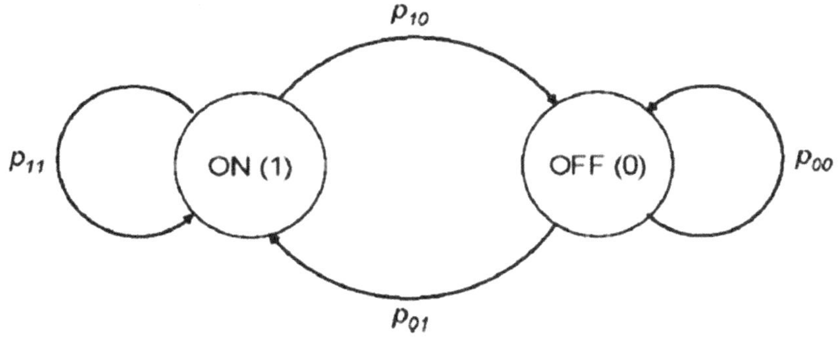

Figure 5.1 LMLC Structure (2 State OFF/ON)

In the OFF (0) state, which mostly consists of Non-Line Of Sight (NLOS)/shadowed, communication failures surpass the current channel correction capabilities, rendering dependable communication impossible. The environment (mean duration of OFF/ON state), vehicle speed, and communication (bit) rate all have an impact on this model's transition likelihood. Transitions between states may be considered taking place at cell limits, where a cubicle represents a segment of data, as the model eliminates short-duration fading events.

Eq. (5.1) specifies the one-step state change matrix, where p_{xy} denotes the transition possibility from x to y. Eq. (5.2) provides the two steady-state alternatives. π_x is represented as the steady-state probability to state x.

$$P = \begin{bmatrix} p_{00} & p_{01} \\ p_{10} & p_{11} \end{bmatrix} \tag{5.1}$$

$$\pi_1 = \frac{p_{01}}{p_{01}+p_{10}};\ \pi_0 = \frac{p_{10}}{p_{01}+p_{10}} \tag{5.2}$$

Eq. (5.3) assumes the two probabilities of transitions, and defines D_x as the average sojourn length of state x for a certain rate of transmission node speed in a given environment. Eq. (5.4) provides $p_x(> n)$ for two states. $p_x(> n)$ is the probability that a designated x persists for more than n time units. The environment that the node or vehicle travels through largely determines the average time in each scenario.

$$p_{10} = \frac{1}{D_1};\ p_{01} = \frac{1}{D_0} \tag{5.3}$$

$$p_0(> n) = p_{00}^n;\ p_1(> n) = p_{11}^n \tag{5.4}$$

$$p_{00} = 1 - p_{01};\ p_{11} = 1 - p_{10} \tag{5.5}$$

The particular environment in which the vehicle or node is working determines the average amount of time spent in each condition. An overview of the various habitats, their typical vehicle speeds, and the average lengths of time spent in both favorable and poor conditions is given in Table 5.1.

Table 5.1 Average Period in OFF and ON Conditions for Various Situations

	City	Out-of-town	Country side	Main road
Speed of vehicle	< 50.1 km/hr	< 50.1 km/hr	60.1 – 70.1 km/hr	< 120.1 km/hr
ON state (1) Period: D_1	22.01 s	8.01 s	16.1 s	18.1 s
OFF state (0) Period: D_0	15.01 s	2.1 s	4.1 s	2.1 s

5.2.2 Communication of Satellite

For every transmitted segment, the satellite downlink communication uses well-known error-correction algorithms. It is anticipated that existing error-correcting methods would be sufficient for perfect communication even in the face of extreme fading and shadowing. Due to substantial fading and shadowing, time variation is used to mitigate the impacts of segment losses. Either a part of intra-user or inter-user inclosing, or both, may succeed. This facilitates the use of error correction and the distribution of the fault across many users or sessions. We may assume that subsequent data user segments are self-governing of one another, as interleaving removes the effect of sequential losses. This analysis of segment rates under different topologies is made easier by this assumption. Unless otherwise noted, the sections that are discussed or shown next to one another in the remainder of the article are sequential sections of a session and are not necessarily transmitted twice. Higher-layer approaches (explained below) increase the chances of recovery.

5.2.3 Analysis of Independence

This proposed approach provides an equation that illustrates the level of dependency between two subsequent portions of a single transmission session after using the segment interleaving technique. To prevent a single satellite failure from causing consecutive losses for a single session at a time, the enclosing objective approach involves scattering a subdivision's sessions. The quantity of Markov describes the changes that occur between two consecutive sessions of a segment's broadcast. The Markov model's d-step transition matrix is denoted by P^d.

$$P^{(d)} = P^d = \begin{bmatrix} p_{00}^d & p_{01}^d \\ p_{10}^d & p_{11}^d \end{bmatrix} \quad (5.7)$$

In Eq. (5.7), p_{ij}^{d} is the probability of a d-step alteration from i to j. According to the fixed state analysis, p_{00}^{d} and p_{10}^{d} will gradually converge to π_0 as the value of d increases, whereas p_{01}^{d} and p_{11}^{d} will ultimately converge to π_1. As a result, the degree of reliance after a d-step state change may be explained as follows:

$$P_{dependent} = \left(\frac{p_{00}^{d}+p_{10}^{d}}{\pi_0}\right) + \left(\frac{p_{01}^{d}+p_{11}^{d}}{\pi_1}\right) \tag{5.8}$$

$P_{dependent} < \delta$, the degree of dependency between two successive sessions, must be smaller than a predetermined value to use the interleaving strategy. By modifying the interleaving value, d, we may meet this need.

Since there are no closed-form solutions for the d-step probability of transitions in Eq. (5.8), we may try $d = 1,2,\ldots$ to determine the proper values of $P_{dependent}$ until the condition $P_{dependent} < \delta$ is met.

5.3 CONCEPT OF ARCHITECTURE

The environment is free of high-shadow losses. We look at the first deployment phase of VANET, when there will be one car per km and a rather thin network in a highway environment. There won't be any noticeable effects from a tiny network with a very low vehicle density when compared to traffic congestion conditions (45 vehicles/km).

5.3.1 Expectations

A few basic assumptions form the foundation of our plan. First, cars will have GPS receivers on them, which will enable them to record the accurate positions and pass the information about the trajectory to the RSU. Second, vehicles may receive satellite transmissions. Third, RSUs have information on the exact positions of other RSUs and have access to a virtual map of the working zone. It should be mentioned that the GPS satellite reception is usually less degraded compared to links of satellite transmission. Each RSU will be connected by a proxy web service to be able to obtain map updates sent to it by an intermediate server. The RSU deployments are supposed to be rare since they will be installed permanently. As a result, the gaps between updates of maps will be greater due to the small amount of RSUs, as well as due to the low frequency of changes of states, but these updates may not be very conspicuous.

5.3.2 Simple Knowledge

In V2R communication, a car asks for internet data when it connects to a nearby RSU. This request includes the vehicle's speed, location, and direction of travel. In particular, during the initial disposition of the VANET, when vehicle density is relatively low (≤1 vehicle/km), the RSU uses this information to predict the possible time for connection and determine the likely next RSU, guaranteeing a manageable load for RSUs. The RSU may handle the request directly if there is still a lot of connection delay. Subsequent answers are sent to the next RSU in the vehicle's path when it leaves the current RSU's coverage. Once the vehicle enters its service area, the subsequent RSU will continue to provide material if the distance between successive RSUs is reasonable, which is usual in urban areas.

However, a satellite downlink channel will be used to enhance content delivery in situations when there is a considerable distance between RSUs, particularly in rural regions where RSUs are widely separated. The satellite downlink option is the main topic of the study.

The vehicle is unable to broadcast acknowledgments when it is moving between two RSUs in the satellite downlink-only region. Adaptive and delayed TCP timeouts will be predicted based on the next RSU's location and used appropriately to preserve TCP connections and avoid needless retransmissions. Selective acknowledgments will be used to avoid needless retransmissions due to the significant downlink delays.

5.3.3 Choices

Four different approaches are addressed to data transfer between satellites and automobiles, namely Forward Error Correction (FEC), which serves as a baseline method, repeated transmission, and fault location prediction and avoidance. Both approaches exhibit different levels of overhead, delay, and unreliable error-handling capabilities.

5.3.3.1 V2V Connection Enhancements

There are many methods that can be used to leverage V2V communication to enhance the effectiveness of the above processes.

5.3.3.2 Recovery of Local Error

They can have vehicles that store data that is to be transferred to other cars in case multiple cars share the same satellite channel in a particular location. The controlled amount of data that has been stored is the storage capacity and the duration of the caching. A repeating buffer can also be used, in which case the oldest data entries are overwritten when the buffer is full. Hash tables can be used to get rapid indexing. When leaving a failed transmission area, a vehicle can send a Negative Acknowledgement (NAK) signal to the next vehicle, which will then retransmit the desirable packet out of its cache.

5.3.3.3 ACK/NAK Relay

Another strategy is the cars moving in opposite directions passing the NAK messages to the RSU that comes before them. The car does not have to wait till it arrives at the next RSU to tell it of a dropped packet; the packet can be resent through satellite. The use of V2V communication as a reverse channel to convey all the selected ACKs and NAKs might increase the usefulness of this tactic even more.

5.3.3.4 Retransmission Relay

Vehicles going in the other direction may also retransmit missed packets to the next RSU. In this situation, it is necessary to guarantee the security of deceitful greetings.

5.3.3.5 Options Comparison

The options offered in the sections above provide different levels of mistake tolerance at the price of delays and administrative expenses. The efficiency (error intolerance) and cost (overheads and delays) should be the factors to consider when choosing the solution; moreover, some options are more fitting in a specific situation compared to others. The simple design is with a simple ACK/NAK to enhance error detection and movement. Though this approach does not require any overhead, communication might not be finished until the vehicle reaches the next RSU. This type of structural design is appropriate where there is no significant spread of RSUs.

Proactive retransmission of the suspected missing segments is considered error site prediction and prevention. Latency and overhead of this system are low. The FEC-based architecture offers a smaller latency but at a higher cost. It is appropriate when the state times that are undesired are in the FEC limits and the faults are randomized.

Constant-time broadcasting is an extremely aggressive trick, which is particularly effective in the case of long periods of evil, yet at the cost of a significant amount of overhead and mediocre delay. A comparison is made of the success rates of various structural designs. It is noteworthy that recurrent broadcasting ($n = 2$) works almost as well as incorrect position predicting ($p_d = 0.9$).

5.4 EVALUATION

To validate our findings and evaluate the performance of various architectural alternatives, simulations were conducted as part of our analysis. The scenario assumed that the node or vehicle was now traversing an area that was exclusively serviced by satellite downlink transmission and had previously requested a file or content via an RSU. This "satellite downlink-only region" was the main focus of our investigation, which limited the simulations to this region. Because RSUs were placed at considerable distances and there were no intermediate RSUs, the highway environment under examination had an uneven distribution of one RSU per 20 kilometers. The LMSC model covered in Section 5.3 served as the foundation for the satellite downlink operational model. The collection of simulation parameters that might be taken into account while creating a simulation model for a satellite-operated VANET is shown in Table 5.2. When constructing the Satellite-VANET communication model, these parameters are utilized to assess various algorithms for the Satellite-VANET framework.

Table 5.2 Simulation Parameters

Parameters	Values
Simulation platform	NS-2
Coding language used	TCL, OTCL, and C++
R_{Time}	50 seconds
Search time	0 – 2.4 sec
No. of nodes	50 – 400
Interface priority queue	Drop tail
Antenna use	Patch antenna
Data transmission range	100 m
Mean size of message generated	256 kilobytes
Memory buffer/node	75 packets

Ten to fifty segments make up the segmented file size. A single Markov state with a duration of one millisecond is represented by each segment. In good condition, a segment is sent without errors, whereas in a poor state, it is lost. A Poisson distribution with parameter λ governs the time intervals between successive segment broadcasts by a node or vehicle. One lakh simulation run was performed for every file. One generated Markov chain model for the satellite channel was used for each thousand simulation runs.

In terms of error position estimation and avoidance at an anticipated rate of detection $(P_d) = 0.9$, the performance assessment is comparable to repeating transmission but has a minimum overhead. Table 5.3 displays the transmission durations and segment loss probability for various topologies.

- The probability that the lost portions will be less than or equal to a certain cost is denoted by "a".
- "b" indicates the probability that the file transfer time will be less than or equal to a specified value (normalized using the mean transfer time of the baseline architecture).

Table 5.3 Transmission Time

Vehicle transmission time	BL	Repeated	P_d	FEC
0.00	0.15	0.45	0.45	0.70
0.05	0.40	0.55	0.70	0.90
0.10	0.55	0.65	0.84	0.90
0.20	0.65	0.74	0.88	0.92
0.25	0.75	0.84	0.90	0.95
0.30	0.80	0.88	0.92	0.97

Table 5.4 shows the potential for transmission section loss for BL, Repeated, P_d, and FEC over a range of transmission periods (t). When compared to repeated transmission strategies, the data clearly show how successful the error location estimate strategy is. Furthermore, these results validate the effectiveness of various architectural alternatives in real-world situations by providing empirical evidence for their unique characteristics. The results show that the error location estimating method is superior to repeated transmission. These findings also support the distinctive visuals of different architectural solutions.

Table 5.4 Transmission Section Loss Prospects

Transmission time (t)	BL	Repeated	P_d	FEC
0.60	0.15	0.17	0.18	0.18
0.90	0.20	0.55	0.70	0.90
1.15	0.50	0.65	0.80	0.90
1.40	0.70	0.74	0.90	0.90
1.65	0.90	1.00	1.00	1.00
1.90	1.00	1.00	1.00	1.00
2.15	1.00	1.00	1.00	1.00
2.40	1.00	1.00	1.00	1.00

5.5 SUMMARY

This chapter provided a method for giving automotive systems internet access, especially during the initial installation stage and in locations with very poor roadside connections. Because it only uses a few RSUs and satellite receive-only stations, the method is practical and economical. It also discussed the context-based error-handling techniques. We examined these options using modeling and quantitative analysis, and our collective evaluations were in agreement. We can further enhance the efficiency of the solution by employing a variety of V2V communication methods. Request-response applications benefit greatly from the technique when a small request yields a substantial amount of return data. Because the method does not provide a continuous connection, active or continuously demanding applications, like IP telephony, are not supported. Additionally, the technology is not designed to support time-sensitive security applications that need massive data flows from automobiles; however, it does support non-time-sensitive or visible safety applications, such as weather, certificate withdrawal list transmission, danger situations, local news, or additional safety alerts via satellites.

CHAPTER 6

IMPROVED VANET CONNECTIVITY IN SPARSE RSU ENVIRONMENTS USING ENHANCED DSR PROTOCOL: CHALLENGES AND SOLUTIONS

6.1 INTRODUCTION

RSUs are essential for VANETs as they facilitate communication between infrastructure and vehicles, enabling data exchange for intelligent transportation systems. However, RSU deployment is limited in rural areas due to high costs and inadequate equipment, leading to communication interruptions. This phase examines adjustments to the DSR protocol to enhance VANET connectivity in low-density RSU networks and addresses traditional RSU communication challenges. It evaluates DSR's on-demand routing effectiveness in establishing V2V and V2I links, analyzing metrics like PDR, network speed, latency, and route stability in simulations. An improved DSR model incorporating satellite-assisted communications is proposed to mitigate intermittent connectivity issues. Results demonstrate that DSR routing, with adaptive selection and multi-hop relaying, significantly improves communication reliability, although challenges such as route-finding latency and packet overhead persist. Potential advancements like edge-assisted computation and hybrid routing algorithms are suggested to enhance VANET performance in rural and highway contexts, aiming for more reliable and scalable vehicular networks.

6.1.1 Design Issues

RSUs are vital in VANETs because they offer fixed communication points for drivers to access the network, receive information, and converse with other automobiles via V2V communication. However, due to the high cost of installation and maintenance, RSU coverage is often limited in rural areas and along roads, resulting in frequent network failures and connection gaps. In a sparsely installed RSU environment, the DSR protocol effectively addresses these issues and enhances connection. When using the DSR protocol to increase VANET connection in sparse RSU locations, several issues must be addressed, including unreliable network connectivity and concealed nodes.

6.1.2 Contributions

Despite several improvements to VANET routing protocols, present research has yet to completely solve the issues of combining DSR with sparse RSU situations while retaining low latency and high packet delivery rates. The primary contributions of this research phase are:

1. Assessing the influence of RSU sparsity on VANET performance and evaluating DSR-based routing in such scenarios.
2. Suggesting a better DSR model with satellite-assisted communication to address connection difficulties.
3. Evaluating the balance between control overhead, route finding delay, and network stability in low-density vehicle networks.

6.2 IMPACT OF RSU SPARSITY ON VANET

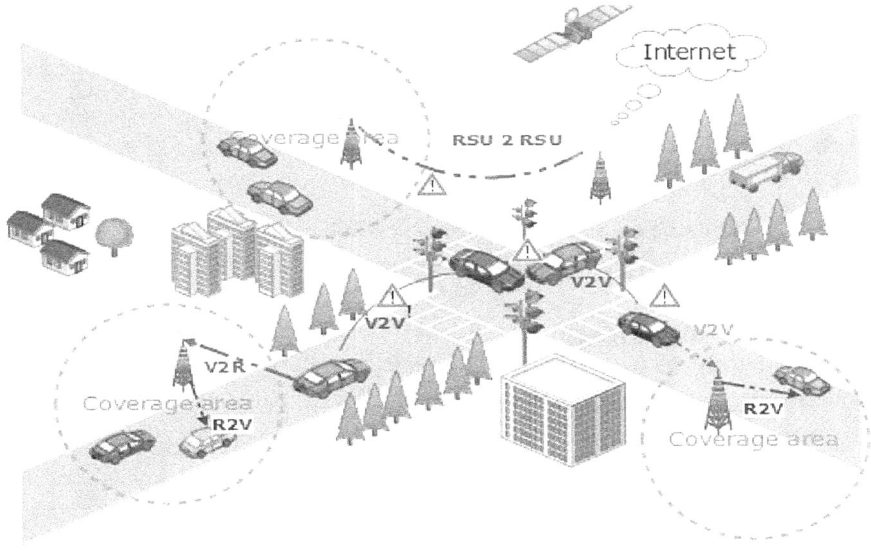

Figure 6.1 Analyzing Impact of RSU Sparsity on VANET Performance and DSR-Based Routing in Such Environments

From Figure 6.1, the following components are described briefly.

V2V:

- Red arrows between cars at the intersection.

- Vehicles communicate directly with each other to exchange information like speed, position, and warnings (e.g., accident ahead, emergency braking).

V2R:

- Green arrows showing vehicles connecting to RSUs.
- Vehicles send/receive information from RSUs, such as traffic signal status, road conditions, or alerts.

RSU-to-Vehicle (R2V):

- RSUs send alerts, traffic updates, or environmental data to the vehicles.
- Highlighted in orange coverage areas around the RSUs.

RSU-to-RSU Communication:

- Shown in a blue dashed line between RSUs.
- RSUs share data between them to coordinate and provide consistent information across a network.

Internet/GNSS Satellite Link:

- RSUs are connected to the Internet via satellite, enabling global communication and access to cloud data or services.

6.3 PROPOSED METHODOLOGY

Step 1: Baseline DSR Implementation

- Execute basic DSR protocol

The DSR protocol is used in this research to improve communication reliability and connectivity in VANETs, especially when sparse RSU deployment is involved. The process entails setting up a simulation environment to evaluate DSR's performance and expanding its capabilities to handle typical VANET issues like high node mobility and route breakages.

Simulation Environment

NS-2 (or NS-3/OMNeT++), which has integrated support for DSR and adaptable mobility models, is used to run the simulation. The SUMO is used to produce the vehicle movement, which simulates actual driving patterns on urban and semi-urban road networks.

Simulation Tool: NS-2 (v2.35)

Mobility Tool: SUMO

Routing Protocol: DSR

Number of Vehicles: 50 to 150 nodes

Simulation Area: 1000m × 1000m

RSU Count: 0 (baseline) to 5 (sparse deployment)

Vehicle Speed: 10–50 km/h

Simulation Time: 300 seconds

6.3.1 DSR Protocol Implementation

- **Route Discovery:** A source broadcasts the RREQ when it wants a path to a destination. Unless they have a legitimate path to the destination, nodes that receive the RREQ forward it.
- **Route Reply:** The RREP is sent by the destination or an intermediary node that has a valid route.
- **Route Maintenance:** The RERR packets are used to identify broken links, which cause the source to start a fresh route discovery.

6.3.2 Protocol Setup in Simulation

- The built-in components of the simulation tool are used to enable DSR in Figure 6.1. Vehicles are set up for V2V communication via DSR. Figure 6.2 illustrates how RSUs are modeled as stationary nodes with wireless communication capability.

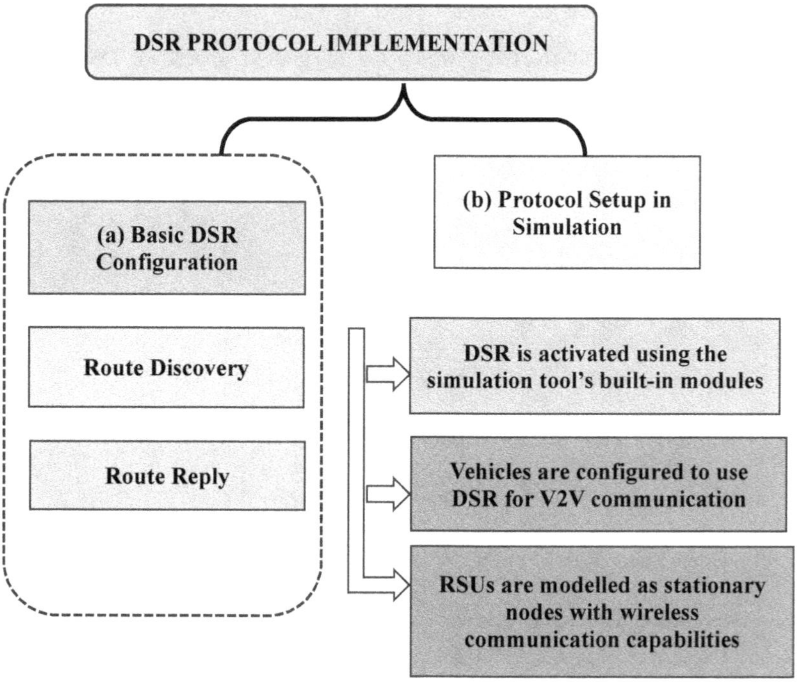

Figure 6.2 DSR Protocol Implementation

6.3.3 Mobility and Traffic Modelling

SUMO-generated mobility traces simulate realistic vehicle trajectories.

Figure 6.3 simulates time-sensitive data transfers between infrastructure and automobiles by generating communication traffic using UDP/CBR. The testing of varying vehicle densities reflects different traffic circumstances. Examine its performance in scenarios with limited RSU coverage.

Step 1: Mobility and traffic modelling

Step 2: Identification of Challenges

- Frequent Route Breakages
- High latency in route discovery
- Increased routing overhead
- Packet drops due to short V2V link lifetimes

Step 3: Proposed Enhancements to DSR

a) Caching with Mobility Prediction

- Nodes predict neighbour movement using GPS and maintain a cache of stable links.

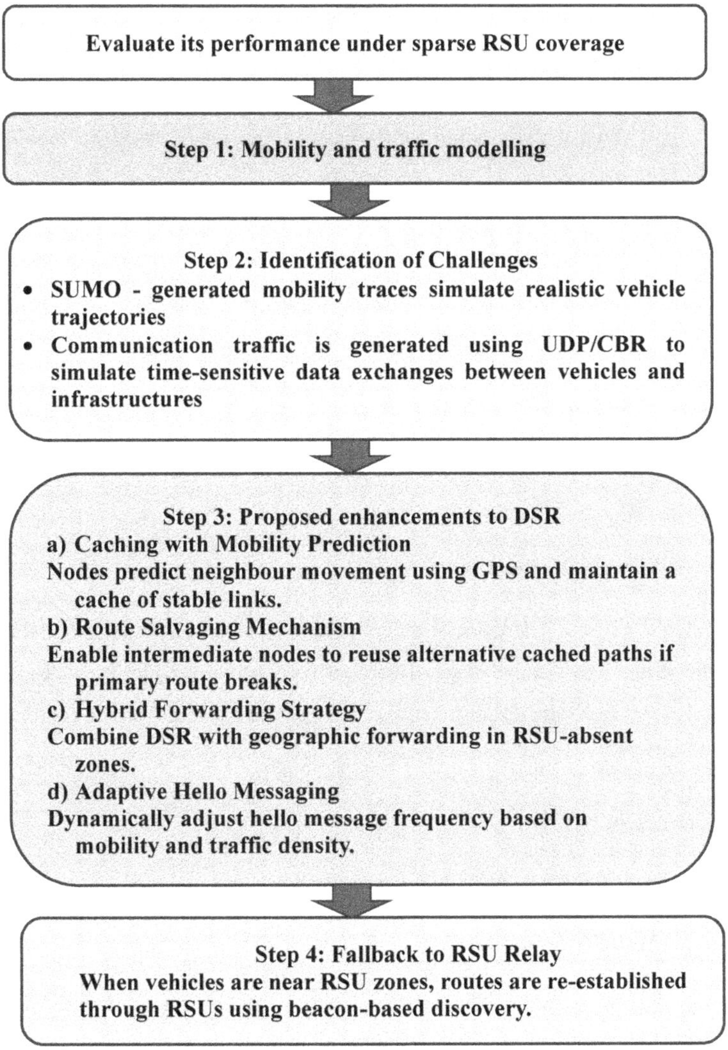

Figure 6.3 Mobility and Traffic Modelling

b) Route Salvaging Mechanism

- Enable intermediate nodes to reuse alternative cached paths if primary route breaks.

c) Hybrid Forwarding Strategy

- Combine DSR with geographic forwarding in RSU-absent zones.

d) Adaptive Hello Messaging

- Dynamically adjust hello message frequency based on mobility and traffic density.

Step 4: Fallback to RSU Relay

- When vehicles are near RSU zones, routes are re-established through RSUs using beacon-based discovery.

6.4 RESULTS AND DISCUSSION

Mathematical Framework: Enhancing VANET Connectivity Using DSR in Sparse RSU Scenarios.

(i) Network Model

Let the VANET network be modelled as a dynamic graph $G(V, E)$, where V is the set of vehicles and RSUs and E is set of wireless links between nodes (vehicles or RSUs). Each edge $e_{ij} \in E$exists if the distance between nodes i and j is less than the communication range RRR.

$$e_{\{ij\}} \in E \iff d(i,j) \leq R \tag{6.1}$$

In Eq. (6.1), $d(i,j)$ is the Euclidean distance between node i and node j.

(ii) Mobility Model

Utilize the Random Waypoint Model or SUMO-generated traces. All vehicles travel with speed $v_i(t) \in [v_{min}, v_{max}]$. Vehicle location over time is determined as:

$$x_{i(t)} = x_{i(t-\Delta t)} + v_{i(t)} \cdot cos(\theta_{i(t)}) \cdot \Delta t \tag{6.2}$$

$$y_{i(t)} = y_{i(t-\Delta t)} + v_{i(t)} \cdot sin(\theta_{i(t)}) \cdot \Delta t \tag{6.3}$$

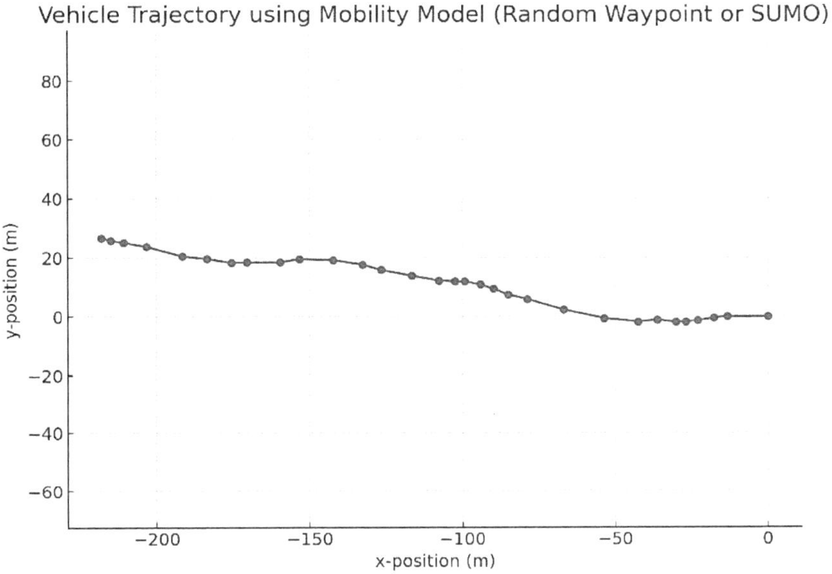

Figure 6.4 Trajectory Graph of a Vehicle Using the Mobility Model

Similar to behavior from Random Waypoint or SUMO-generated traces, Figure 6.4 displays a vehicle's trajectory graph utilizing the mobility model over time with a random speed between 10 and 50 km/h and slight directional shifts.

(iii) Route Lifetime Estimation

Given node mobility, the expected lifetime of a link *T_{link}* between nodes i and j is:

T_{{link}} ≈ 1/{R − d(i,j)}{|v_i − v_j| (6.4)

This is utilized to estimate path stability and trigger caching/route salvaging in DSR.

(iv) PDR

$$\text{PDR} = \frac{P_{\text{received}}}{P_{\text{sent}}} \times 100\% \tag{6.5}$$

In Eq. (6.5), P_{received} is the number of packets received at destination and P_{sent} is the number of packets sent from source.

(v) Average E2E Delay

$$D_{\text{avg}} = \frac{1}{N}\sum_{i=1}^{N}\left(t_{\text{receive},i} - t_{\text{send},i}\right) \tag{6.6}$$

In Eq. (6.6), N is the number of successfully delivered packets, $t_{\text{receive},i}$ is the time at i-th packet was received, and $t_{\text{send},i}$ is the time at i-th packet was sent.

Table 6.1 Simulation Results under Varying RSU Counts

RSU Count	PDR (%)	E2E Delay (ms)	Routing Overhead (%)
0	61	210	45
1	73	160	38
3	84	115	32
5	91	90	27

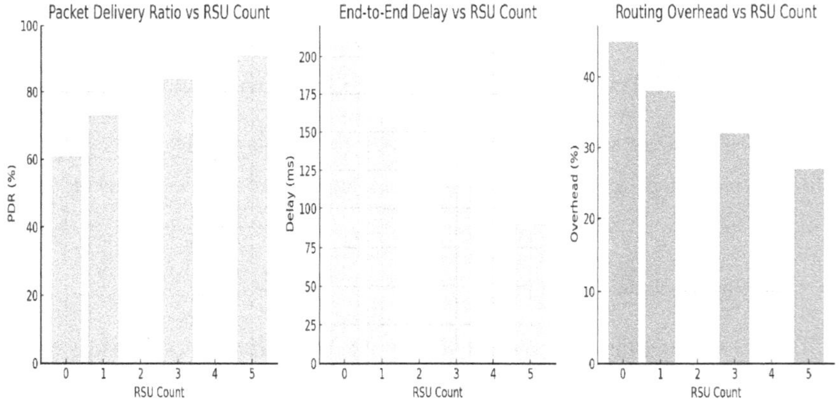

Figure 6.5 Comparative results of PDR, ETE and Routing Overhead Vs RSU Count

Even a modest number of RSUs may significantly improve network performance in a VANET, as shown in Table 6.1. Delivery dependability, latency, and control overhead all show improvements. This bolsters the notion that hybrid communication models, such as V2V with infrastructure, are more successful, particularly in settings that are dynamic or only partly linked. Figure 6.5 displays the comparative outcomes of the parameters, including PDR, E2E delay, and routing overhead.

6.5 SUMMARY

This chapter shows the possibility of improving the DSR protocol to enhance vehicular communication in contexts with sparse RSU deployment. We discovered significant drawbacks of conventional DSR in VANETs, including frequent route breakages, high latency, and increased routing overhead as a result of quick topology changes, by using SUMO to simulate actual urban traffic patterns and NS-2 to assess performance. We implemented several improvements, such as route salvaging techniques, adaptive hello messaging, mobility-aware caching, and hybrid forwarding algorithms, to solve these problems. Even when RSUs are absent or sparse, our findings show that these changes greatly enhance network performance, particularly in terms of PDR, decreased E2E latency, and decreased routing overhead. A hybrid approach for VANET communication that makes use of both infrastructure and ad hoc capabilities is validated by the addition of backup routing via RSUs, which further improves connection when it is available. All things considered, the improved DSR protocol presents a viable way to preserve reliable and effective communication in dynamic vehicle situations with no infrastructure assistance.

CHAPTER 7

A NOVEL TECHNIQUE OF ỌDỊGBO METAHEURISTIC ALGORITHM BASED OPTIMIZED ENERGY-EFFICIENT AND RELIABLE ROUTING PROTOCOL FOR VANETS TO AUGMENT QOS CONDITIONS

7.1 INTRODUCTION

VANETs are a subset of mobile wireless networks in which vehicles function as intelligent, self-organizing nodes capable of interacting without permanent infrastructure. Because of their high mobility and constantly changing architecture, VANETs endure frequent connection breakdowns, unpredictable connectivity, and varying node density, making effective communication and route stability very difficult. Unlike traditional ad hoc networks, automotive nodes produce dynamic traffic patterns, which often result in higher routing overhead, packet collisions, and unequal energy consumption. Furthermore, with short connection lifetimes and quickly changing network circumstances, sustaining reliable multi-hop communication becomes problematic. These distinct qualities need routing techniques that are adaptable, energy-efficient, and resistant to mobility and topological changes. Because existing routing strategies frequently experience high delays, packet loss, and resource imbalances, the development of optimized, intelligent routing techniques has emerged as a critical research focus for improving the overall performance and communication reliability of VANET environments.

7.1.1 Design Issues

Previous studies have thoroughly examined VANET problems from a variety of perspectives. Although it provided a basis for safe communication, it lacked energy-aware, adaptive routing techniques and instead concentrated on security architectures and threat mitigation. The EVMRP was suggested to improve routing by incorporating speed and energy factors; however, it was not intelligently optimized and experienced packet loss in dynamic settings. Due to its dependence on static maps, LCGL enhanced geographic link connectivity, but its performance suffered in areas with significant movement or a large concentration of obstacles. ACO and clustering were integrated into bus-based VANETs for multipath routing;

however, since their method relied on relay selection and route probability computations, it was complicated and latency-intensive.

7.1.2 Contributions

This research phase proposes a new intelligent and energy-aware CH selection in VANETs. The innovation of this phase is its unified approach to both CH and route selection inside a single optimization framework, which considerably improves flexibility in highly dynamic VANET situations. The main contributions are the following:

1. A new hybrid routing framework using the OMOA is suggested. This protocol uses metaheuristic optimization, machine learning-based route scoring, and probabilistic filtering to improve routing efficiency and dependability.
2. This model combines M-ELA with an RF classifier for intelligent route prediction and prioritizing.
3. Additionally, the Bloom filter is utilized to reduce duplicate transmissions and increase communication efficiency.
4. Moreover, the OMOA fine-tunes routing parameters by repeatedly refining possible CH configurations via directed learning and adaptive exploration. The optimization method is directed by a multi-objective fitness function that takes into account residual energy, distance to sink, intra-cluster distance, and node connection, resulting in optimum CH and route selection.

7.2 PROPOSED METHODOLOGY

7.2.1 Network Model

Sink Node Location: To gather aggregated data from CHs, a static sink node (BS) is placed in the middle or periphery of the deployment zone. Its computing capability is larger, and its energy is limitless.

Initial Energy: Energy consumption is based on the first-order radio model, which takes into account both transmission and reception costs. All sensor nodes start with the same amount of energy (E_0).

Mobility Model: Based on Gauss-Markov or random waypoint mobility models, vehicles move according to patterns seen in the actual world.

Communication Assumptions: Depending on how far away they are from the CH or sink, nodes may communicate in a single-hop or multi-hop fashion. Every node has a fixed radio communication range (e.g., 100 m).

Following the identification of optimum CHs using OMOA and the scoring of candidate paths using the M-ELA and RF, the bloom filter is used in this routing architecture to remove duplicate or repetitive packets before transmission. This guarantees that only distinct and relevant packets are sent across the network. By doing this, the system increases throughput overall, reduces needless retransmissions, and saves node energy. Mobility or a poor signal may cause packet loss, and retransmission is handled quickly. Due to inconsistent workload over time, the sensor nodes have heterogeneous residual energy but uniform capabilities.

7.2.2 Euclidean Distance Computation

For energy and routing calculations, Euclidean distance between any two nodes i and j is computed as:

$$d_{ij} = \sqrt{(x_i - x_j)^2 + (y_i - y_j)^2} \tag{7.1}$$

This function is essential for routing choices where the shortest or most energy-efficient lines are selected, as well as for CH selection based on distance to the centroid or BS.

7.2.3 Energy Dissipation Model

The first-order radio model, which is often used in WSN, is the energy model in use. A node's energy expenditure while sending an l-bit message across a distance d is represented as follows:

$$E_{tx}(l,d) = \begin{cases} lE_{elec} + l_{\epsilon f_s} d^2, & d < d_0 \\ lE_{elec} + l_{\epsilon_{mp}} d^4 & d \geq d_0 \end{cases} \tag{7.2}$$

In Eq. (7.2), E_{elec} is the energy consumption per bit for the transmitter and receiver circuitry, ϵf_s is the free space energy coefficient, ϵ_{mp} is the multipath fading energy coefficient and $d_0 = \sqrt{\frac{\epsilon f_s}{\epsilon_{mp}}}$ is the threshold distance between free space and multipath models.

In contrast to more conventional metaheuristics like PSO, ACO, or GWO, OMOA is innovative due to its adaptive mutation technique and directed exploration. OMOA strikes a compromise between exploration and exploitation by adaptively modifying search routes depending on residual energy distribution, connectedness, and cluster compactness. Previous algorithms either overemphasize exploration, which results in sluggish convergence, or exploitation, which puts local optima in danger. The method repeatedly refines these solutions using its multi-objective fitness function (Eq. (7.5)), which takes into account residual energy, intra-cluster distance, connection, and distance to the sink. Each candidate solution represents the CH configuration. The amount of energy used to receive is:

$$E_{rx}(l) = l.E_{elec} \tag{7.3}$$

$$k_{opt} = \sqrt{\frac{N}{2\pi}}.\frac{\sqrt{\epsilon_{fs}}}{\sqrt{\epsilon_{mp}}}.\frac{L}{d_{toBS}^2} \tag{7.4}$$

In Eq. (7.4), d_{toBS}^2 is the average distance from CHs to the BS. This formula balances intra-cluster and inter-cluster energy usage, forming the basis of our energy-aware clustering framework

7.2.4 Proposed Methodology

To overcome the difficulties of high mobility, dynamic topology, and energy restrictions, the suggested system mixes machine learning and bio-inspired optimization to provide an intelligent and energy-efficient routing protocol designed for VANETs, as shown in Figure 7.1. For precise route selection and reliable link classification, the design combines a RF classifier with an M-ELA. OMOA is used to modify routing parameters in real time to further improve routing performance under dynamic network circumstances. A suggested optimization module is used for CH selection based on several factors, including residual energy, node connection, and proximity to RSUs. This module was inspired by the pollination process in flowers. To improve communication efficiency and filter redundant transmissions, a Bloom Filter is also included. In comparison to current protocols like Low-Energy Adaptive Clustering Hierarchy (LEACH), PSO-LEACH, Grey Wolf Optimization (GWO), and ACO, the system exhibits higher performance in terms of PDR, energy consumption, latency, and network stability when assessed by comprehensive simulations under various traffic loads and mobility models.

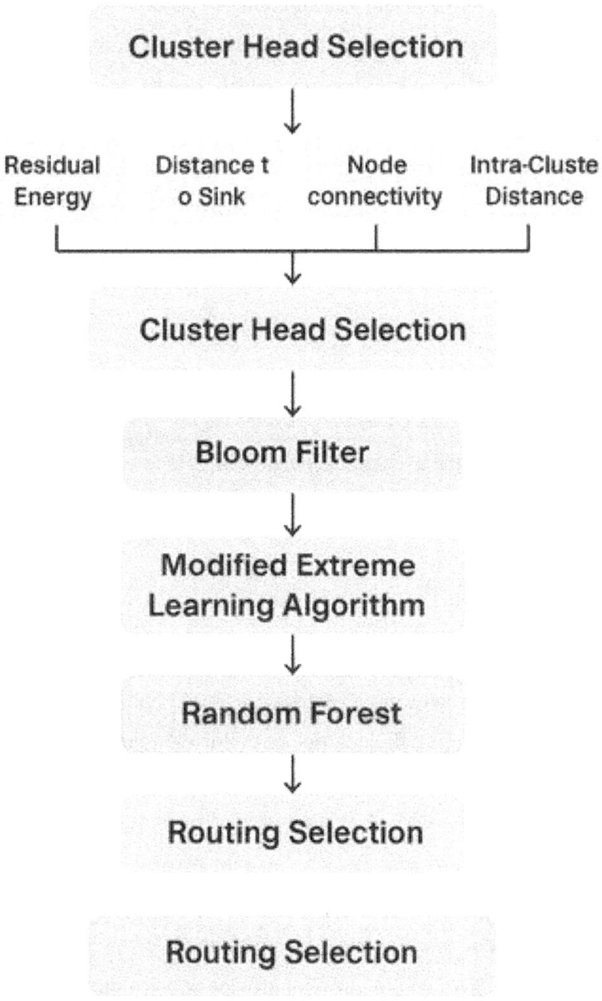

Figure 7.1 Flowchart of Route Selection in Proposed Model

7.2.5 CH Selection Criteria

Rather than random or probabilistic CH selection model utilizes proposed optimization to select CHs based on residual energy $E_i(t)$, intra-cluster distance d_{ic} – distance from node to centroid, distance to BS $d_{i,bs}$, and node connectivity degree δ_i. The CH fitness function is:

$$F_{CH}(i) = \alpha.\frac{E_i(t)}{E_0} + \beta.\left(1 - \frac{d_{ic}}{d_{max}}\right) + \gamma.\left(1 - \frac{d_{i,bs}}{d_{max}}\right) + \theta.\frac{\delta_i}{\delta_{max}} \quad (7.5)$$

In Eq. (7.5), $\alpha, \beta, \gamma, \theta$ are the weight coefficients satisfying $\alpha + \beta + \gamma + \theta = 1$, d_{max} is the maximum possible distance in the network, and δ_{max} is the maximum degree observed in the network.

- Residual energy: This guarantees that the CH selection prevents node depletion too quickly and encourages network-wide energy balance.
- Distance to BS (Sink): this lowers long-range energy drains and communication costs for inter-cluster transfers.
- Node connectivity degree: This improves route stability and lowers link breakage by giving preference to nodes with higher local connectivity.
- Intra-cluster distance: This lowers intra-cluster communication overhead by promoting compact clusters by limiting the average distance between nodes and their CH.

This is a multi-objective fitness function combining energy, topology, and spatial awareness, making CH selection both adaptive and global.

7.2.6 Sensor Node State Transition

To further improve energy savings, nodes switch between Active, Sleep, or Transmit states based on their role (CH or member), proximity to CH, residual energy threshold E_{th}, and data relevance The state transition function is given by:

$$State_i(t+1) = \begin{cases} Active, & E_i(t) > E_{th} \wedge d_{i,CH} < R \\ Sleep, & E_i(t) > E_{th} \wedge d_{i,CH} > R \\ Transmit, & if\ CH\ and\ data\ aggregated \end{cases} \quad (7.6)$$

This where and when logic directly controls node duty cycling to preserve power, reduce congestion, and extend network lifetime. The network initialization includes the following:

1. Deploy N nodes randomly in a $L \times L$ grid.
2. Assign initial energy E_0 to all nodes.
3. Compute pairwise distances d_{ij} and initialize node connectivity matrix.
4. Estimate k_{opt} for optimal cluster count.

5. Initiate CH selection via proposed optimization
6. Form clusters and establish TDMA-based communication schedules.

Pseudocode: of proposed algorithm in Sensor Node State Transition

```
Input:
N → Number of nodes (vehicles)
E0 → Initial energy for each node
T → Total simulation time / rounds
Sink → Static Base Station location
Thresholds → Energy, delay, distance thresholds
Output:
Optimized routes with minimum delay, high PDR, and energy efficiency
Begin
1. Initialize network:
   – Randomly deploy N mobile nodes in 2D space
   – Set energy E0 for each node
   – Assign communication range and mobility mode
2. For each round t in T:
   2.1. Calculate features for each node:
      – Residual energy
      – Node degree (connectivity)
      – Distance to sink
      – Link stability (mobility factor)
   2.2. Apply Random Forest:
      – Train RF classifier with historical data
      – Predict reliability score for each node
   2.3. Select CHs using M – ELA:
      – Initialize random weights for ELA
      – Compute output matrix using single – hidden layer
```

$- \ Optimize\ weights\ for\ energy\ and\ coverage$

$- \ Select\ top\ nodes\ as\ CHs\ based\ o\ output\ scores$

2.4. $Optimize\ CHs\ and\ routing\ parameters\ using\ PSO$:

$- \ Define\ fitness\ function$: $maximize\ PDR, minimize\ delay\ and\ energy$

$- \ Update\ position\ and\ velocity\ of\ particles\ (candidate\ CH\ sets)$

$- \ Select\ global\ best\ CHs\ and\ routing\ configuration$

2.5. $Apply\ Bloom\ Filter$:

$- \ Maintain\ compact\ list\ of\ recently\ transmitted\ packet\ IDs$

$- \ Filter\ out\ duplicate\ messages\ at\ node\ level$

$- \ Reduce\ transmission\ overhead$

2.6. $Form\ clusters\ and\ forward\ data$:

$- \ Nodes\ join\ nearest\ CH$

$- \ CH\ aggregates\ and\ forwards\ to\ sink$

$- \ Update\ residual\ energy\ and\ remove\ dead\ nodes$

3. $End\ For$

4. $Output\ performance\ metrics$:

$- \ PDR, delay, CH\ count, lifetime, residual\ energy$

End

7.2.7 Ọdịgbo Metaheuristic Optimization Algorithm

The optimization procedure in this step uses the OMOA to choose the best CHs and routing routes in a VANET system. First, a population of potential solutions is produced, each of which stands for a distinct CH arrangement. A multi-objective fitness function based on residual energy, BS distance, intra-cluster compactness, and packet delivery efficiency is used by OMOA to assess each solution. The technique iteratively refines the population toward globally optimum solutions via adaptive mutation and directed exploration. After choosing the best CHs, superfluous or ineffective links are removed using a Bloom filter. M-ELA and RF classifiers are used to further assess and rank the final routing pathways to provide resilient, energy-efficient, and QoS-aware data transfer appropriate for dynamic VANET topologies.

7.2.8 Proposed Odigbo Metaheuristic Optimization Algorithm

The unique OMOA is included in the suggested optimization technique to improve routing and CH selection in a dynamic VANET environment. The OMOA algorithm is a population-based global optimization method that relies on directed search and adaptation mechanisms. Under this model, every particle or candidate solution is used to represent a possible arrangement of CHs and routes. The quality of a candidate is assessed by the use of a multi-objective fitness criterion that simultaneously incorporates residual energy, distance to sink or BS, node connectivity, and cluster compactness.

The OMOA algorithm builds upon the candidate solutions by improving them in a series of adaptive exploration and exploitation steps, hence guaranteeing high load balancing and reduced communication expenses. Classification schemes like the M-ELA and RF classifier are also included to assess the stability and reliability of the possible routes; when added to OMOA, they further increase the resilience in routing. Thus, the suggested methodology will ensure energy-saving and QoS-based communication by focusing on solutions with a high PDR, low energy imbalance, and low latency. These properties make the method appropriate in the context of highly mobile and stochastic topologies of VANETs.

The OMOA, which dynamically finds the best CHs based on a variety of parameters to guarantee stable and energy-efficient clustering in VANET settings, is used to pick CHs in Figure 7.2. A multi-objective fitness function that takes into account residual energy, distance to the BS, intra-cluster distance, and node connection is used by the algorithm to assess each node. To choose the best nodes to serve as CHs, OMOA repeatedly searches the search space using adaptive directed learning. This balances energy usage and enhances cluster stability.

By lowering the frequency of re-clustering and guaranteeing effective data aggregation within clusters, this clever CH selection procedure greatly extends network lifespan and promotes dependable communication. To choose the best characteristics from the input dataset, the research effort offers an OMOA, which will be described in the next section.

(1) Represents the solution $Mazi$ when using the decision variables and D dimensions in the MOA model.

$$Mazi = [x_1, x_2, x_3, \dots, x_D] \tag{7.7}$$

The fitness charge of each Mazi will be calculated as a vector of (2);

$$f(Mazi) = f(x_1, x_2, x_3, \dots, x_D) \tag{7.8}$$

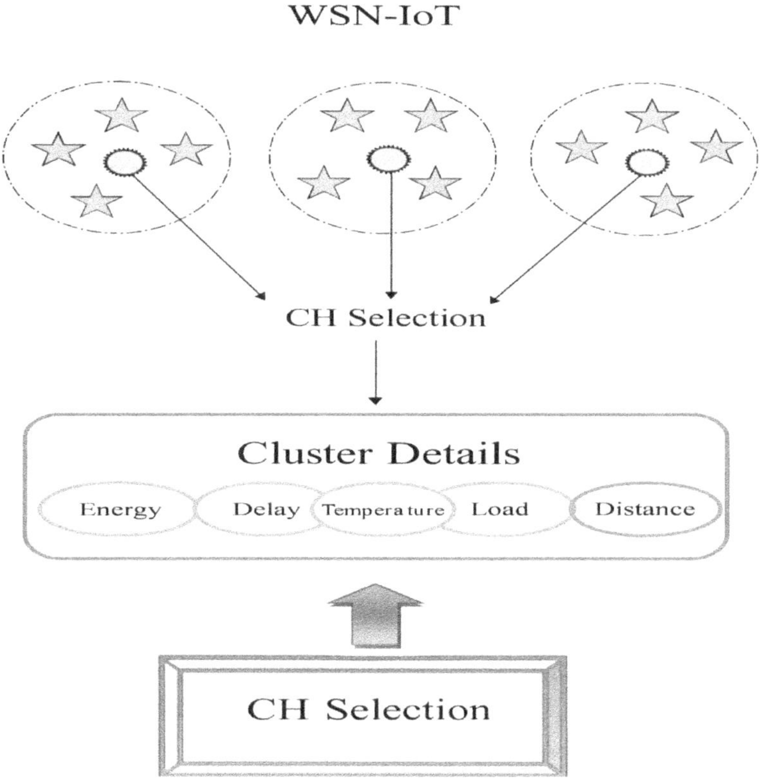

Figure 7.2 Working Process of CH Selection

Pseudocode: of OMOA for VANET Routing

Input:

$N \leftarrow$ number of nodes

$Max\_Iter \leftarrow$ maximum number of iterations

$Pop\_Size \leftarrow$ population size

$\alpha, \beta, \gamma, \theta \leftarrow$ fitness weights (for energy, distance, PDR, cluster balance)

$Constraints \leftarrow$ transmission range, energy limits, etc.

Output:

Optimal Cluster Head Set and Routing Paths

```
Begin
1. Initialize Population of candidate solutions (CH sets) randomly
2. For each solution in the population:
    Evaluate Fitness:
      Fitness = α × ResidualEnergy +
            β × (1 / DistanceToBS) +
            γ × PDR +
            θ × ClusterBalance
3. Set best_solution ← best fitness in population
4. iter ← 1
5. While iter ≤ Max_Iter do:
    For each solution Xi in population:
      Generate New Candidate X' using directional exploration:
        If rand < p_direction:
          X' ← GuidedUpdate(Xi, best_solution)
        Else:
          X' ← RandomPerturbation(Xi)
      Evaluate Fitness(X')
      If Fitness(X') > Fitness(Xi):
        Replace Xi with X'
    Update best_solution if any improved
    iter ← iter + 1
6. Apply Bloom Filter to reduce redundant paths from selected CHs
7. Classify and prioritize final routing paths using M − ELA + Random Forest
8. Output best_solution as Optimized CHs and Routes
End
```

This age group has some limits, such as (a) a time of irregular eating, sleeping, and desiring habits; a natural propensity towards childishness (including undirected and untargeted energies); and a rush of nostalgic energy in the first few months.

7.2.9 Path Selection for Routing

After choosing the best CH nodes using the OMOA, the suggested VANET routing architecture selects the route path. The quality of accessible routing pathways is scored and predicted using the RF classifier in combination with the M-ELA model. Features including residual energy, connection stability, hop count, and E2E latency are taken into consideration while evaluating each route. To guarantee maximal packet delivery and the least amount of latency, the top-ranked route is constantly chosen. In very dynamic VANET situations, a bloom filter is utilized to remove redundant transmissions, lower communication overhead, and preserve QoS to further improve routing efficiency.

7.2.10 Modified Extreme Learning Algorithm (M-ELA) – Description

M-ELA is an advanced version of standard ELA, tailored for improving learning performance of Single Layer Feedforward neural Networks (SLFNs). M-ELA overcomes these limitations by introducing enhancements in weight initialization, hidden node optimization, and regularization techniques. Specifically, M-ELA:

$$BK = \begin{bmatrix} BK_{1,1} & BK_{1,2} & \cdots & BK_{1,dim} \\ BK_{2,1} & BK_{2,2} & \cdots & BK_{2,dim} \\ \vdots & \vdots & \ddots & \vdots \\ BK_{pop,1} & BK_{pop,2} & \cdots & BK_{pop,dim} \end{bmatrix} \quad (7.9)$$

In Eq. (7.9), pop showcases populace magnitude, pop dimension, $BK_{i,j}$ cabinets jth dimension of ith individual. X_i is specified as:

$$X_i = BK_{lb} + rand(BK_{ub} - BK_{lb}) \quad (7.10)$$

In Eq. (7.10), i showcases an numeral in [1, pop], BK_{lb} besides BK_{ub} showcase limitations, and$rand \in [0, 1]$. The most fitting leader X_L is specified as:

$$f_{best} = \min\left(f(X_i)\right) \quad (7.11)$$

$$X_L = X(find(f_{best} == f(X_i))) \quad (7.12)$$

- Uses data-driven initialization or optimization techniques to select better initial input weights and biases.
- Incorporates activation function tuning or selection strategies to adapt to the nature of the input data.
- Employs regularization (e.g., L2-norm) to control overfitting and improve generalization performance.
- Allows for adaptive hidden layer sizing, choosing the optimal number of neurons based on performance metrics.

Algorithm: OMOA – based Hybrid Routing Protocol for VANETs

Input:

Number of nodes N, *initial energy* E_0

Mobility model (Random Waypoint / Gauss – Markov)

Transmission range R

Simulation parameters (iterations T, *population size* P*)*

Output:

Optimal CHs

Energy – efficient and QoS – aware routing paths

Initialization

1.1 *Deploy* N *vehicular nodes randomly in the network area.*

1.2 *Assign initial energy* E_0 *to each node.*

1.3 *Compute pairwise distances and initialize node connectivity matrix.*

1.4 *Estimate optimal cluster count* K.

Population Generation (OMOA Initialization)

2.1 *Generate initial population of candidate solutions, where each solution encode*

2.2 *Evaluate each candidate using the multi – objective fitness function:*

where residual energy (Eres), distance to BS (dBS), connectivity (Conn), and intra – cluster distance (dintra) are weighted.

OMOA Optimization Process

3.1 *For each iteration* $t = 1$ *to* T:

Apply directional exploration to update candidate CHs.

Use adaptive mutation to avoid local optima.

Evaluate updated solutions with fitness function.

Retain best − performing CH configuration.

Cluster Formation

4.1 *Assign member nodes to nearest CHs.*

4.2 *Apply TDMA − based scheduling for intra − cluster communication.*

Route Prediction (M − ELA + Random Forest)

5.1 *Extract routing features: residual energy, link stability, hop count, delay, pack*

5.2 *Use RF to classify candidate routes into {High, Medium, Low priority}.*

5.3 *Apply M − ELA to score and rank high − priority routes.*

5.4 *Select the top − ranked route for data forwarding.*

Bloom Filter for Redundancy Suppression

6.1 *Maintain a Bloom Filter of recently transmitted packet IDs.*

6.2 *If a packet ID is already present → suppress transmission.*

6.3 *Else → forward packet and update Bloom Filter.*

Data Transmission Phase

7.1 *Member nodes send data to CHs (intra − cluster).*

7.2 *CHs aggregate and forward data via selected routes to the BS.*

Energy Update

8.1 *Update node energies based on the first − order radio model.*

8.2 *If energy ≤ threshold → mark node as dead.*

Reclustering

9.1 *After every Rint rounds, re − run OMOA for CH reselection.*

9.2 *Repeat steps 2 − 8 until simulation ends.*

7.2.11 Random Forest Classifier

Each tree is trained on a random subset of the data (using bootstrapping), which reduces variance. At each node split, a random subset of features is considered, which minimizes correlation among trees and avoids overfitting. The final prediction is made through majority voting (for classification) or averaging (for regression).

$$y_{t+1}^{i,j} = \begin{cases} y_t^{i,j} + n(1 = \sin(r)) \times y_t^{i,j} & p < r \\ y_t^{i,j} + n(2r - 1) \times y_t^{i,j} & else \end{cases} \tag{7.13}$$

$$n = 0.05 \times e^{2\times\left(\frac{t}{T}\right)^2} \tag{7.14}$$

In Eqns. (7.13)-(7.14), $y_t^{i,j}$ and $y_{t+1}^{i,j}$ showcase the sites of dimension, r ∈ [0, 1], p = 0.9, T repetition termination. In the context of VANET routing, the RF classifier is employed to evaluate and rank routing paths based on several features like:

- Link stability
- Residual energy of nodes
- Node connectivity
- Distance to the destination or RSU
- Packet delivery history

7.2.12 Combined Working Process in Routing Decision

M-ELA and the RF classifier are used in the suggested VANET routing framework to intelligently choose and assess the best possible routing routes. This hybrid technique improves decision-making in dynamic and resource-constrained vehicular contexts by using the advantages of both robust classification and quick learning. Vehicle nodes are used to extract network information in real time, including residual energy, connection stability, node degree, mobility pattern, distance to destination, and past packet delivery performance. Two major issues in VANET routing are addressed by the combination of M-ELA and RF: (1) the necessity for quick adaptability to changing topologies and (2) the need for strong categorization of dependable routes under unpredictable circumstances. As an improvement on the classic Extreme Learning Algorithm (ELA), M-ELA adds hidden node selection, efficient weight initialization, and regularization to provide quick learning without overfitting.

As a result, nonlinear interactions between routing variables, including residual energy, connection stability, hop count, and latency, may be swiftly captured. Based on the input characteristics, the RF classifier divides routing pathways into groups such as "High Priority," "Medium Priority," and "Low Priority." This lowers the number of potential routes by early filtering out erratic or energy-inefficient ones. The M-ELA model is trained to score and rank the pathways based on nonlinear interactions of input metrics using the candidate routes that were chosen during the RF stage.

To provide dependable and QoS-aware communication in dynamic VANET settings, route selection is carried out using an innovative hybrid technique that combines an M-ELA with the RF classifier. The routing pathways are assessed and graded according to characteristics, including connection stability, energy availability, and past performance, once the best CHs have been chosen using OMOA. While RF improves decision robustness via ensemble learning, M-ELA quickly learns the underlying traffic patterns.

A bloom filter is also included to prevent redundant transmissions, which lowers routing costs and improves bandwidth use. In highly mobile vehicle contexts, this combination method guarantees the selection of the most stable and efficient routes, increasing PDR and reducing E2E latency.

The behaviour of migration is defined as:

$$y_{t+1}^{i,j} = \begin{cases} y_t^{i,j} + C(0,1) \times (y_t^{i,j} - L_t^j) & F_i < F_{ri} \\ y_t^{i,j} + C(0,1) \times (L_t^i - m \times y_t^{i,j}) & else \end{cases} \tag{7.15}$$

$$m = 2 \times \sin(r + \pi/2) \tag{7.16}$$

In Eqns. (7.15)-(7.16), L_t^j scorer, F_i current site, F_{ri} accidental site, $C(0,1)$ showcases the Cauchy mutation. The Cauchy is defined as a continuous two-metric stochastic distribution that is:

$$f(x,\delta,\mu) = \frac{1}{\pi}\frac{\delta}{\delta^2+(x-\mu)^2} - \infty < x < \infty \tag{7.17}$$

In Eq. (7.17), $\delta = 1$, $\mu = 0$, the likelihood density fitness is specified as:

$$f(x,\delta,\mu) = \frac{1}{\pi}\frac{\delta}{x^2+1} - \infty < x < \infty \tag{7.18}$$

M-ELA is a specially designed feedforward network that adjusts its hidden layer weights to quickly find the best connection between features and route performance. The best path is chosen for packet forwarding based on M-ELA's score. M-ELA dynamically re-evaluates the paths, and RF re-classifies when network circumstances (such as congestion and node mobility) change. To continually increase accuracy and flexibility, performance indicators, including real packet delivery, delay, and energy usage, are supplied back into both models. The ideal quokka location inside a group affects how each quokka's site is updated within that group, as shown by the following equations:

$$D^{new} = \frac{(T+H)}{(0.8 \times D^{old})} + \Delta w \times rand \times \Delta X \tag{7.19}$$

$$X^{new} = X^{old} + D^{new} \times N \tag{7.20}$$

In Eqns. (7.19)-(7.20), D^{old} characterizes the Drought besides its charge among $[0,1]), T$ stands for the temperature ratio, which falls within the range of 0.2 to 0.44, and H for the humidity ratio, which ranges from 0.3 to 0.65. to settled on these ratios since that's the range of temperatures and humidity levels that quokkas can survive. A random number with a value between 0 and represented by rand, Δw is the difference in weight among the leader and quokka i. 1, ΔX characterizes the differences of quokka i, quokka's new site is characterized by X^{new}, while the old site is characterized by X^{old}.

RF guarantees strong, quick categorization with a high tolerance for noisy or insufficient data. For accurate ranking and decision-making, M-ELA incorporates nonlinear modeling and adaptive intelligence. In rapidly evolving VANET settings, the integrated model facilitates dependable, delay-minimized, and energy-efficient routing.

7.3 RESULTS AND DISCUSSION

A simulated environment is used to assess the efficacy of the suggested routing protocol, a hybrid system for energy-efficient cluster-based routing that is inspired by flower pollination and improved by bloom filters. The simulation framework follows settings that are in line with benchmark protocol analysis and conforms to generally recognized standards in WSN research. The OMOA uses adaptive exploration and directed learning to repeatedly refine a population of potential CH configurations. To maximize energy efficiency, connectivity, and routing stability in VANETs for practical deployment, it assesses each solution using a multi-objective fitness function.

This phase demonstrated simulation runtimes within real-time constraints by implementing the framework on an Intel Core i7/Ryzen 7 Python 3.11 environment (Table 7.1). RF is renowned for its low-latency predictions, while M-ELA's quick training allows for quick adaptability. Vehicles can handle lightweight route assessment and filtering in operational VANETs because the majority of computing work (such as OMOA-based CH selection) may be delegated to RSUs or edge nodes, guaranteeing real-time viability. A comprehensive list of these input parameters and their corresponding values is presented in Table 7.1.

Our simulations were run under several mobility models (random waypoint and Gauss–Markov), which simulate both random vehicle movement and more realistic trajectory-based mobility, and over a range of node densities (100, 200, 300, and 500 nodes) to guarantee robustness. To represent real-time data exchange in safety and infotainment applications, we also used CBR sources to vary traffic loads. Variable transmission ranges (25 m), restricted beginning energy (2 J per node), and realistic channel models (free-space and multipath fading) are all reflected in the parameter choices. These circumstances test the flexibility of the suggested protocol in situations with high mobility, heavy traffic, sparseness, and density.

7.3.1 Performance Metrics

- **PDR:** Evaluates routing reliability by measuring the percentage of successfully delivered packets. Our protocol consistently achieves the highest PDR (96.8%, Table 7.4), reflecting robustness under dynamic conditions.
- **E2E Delay:** Measures the time taken for data to travel from source to destination. With a delay of 140 ms, the proposed model ensures timely delivery, which is critical for safety-related VANET applications.
- **Energy Consumption & Residual Energy:** Track how efficiently nodes utilize energy. As shown in Table 7.2, our model achieves the lowest total energy consumption (104 J) and the highest residual energy (0.95 J), demonstrating balanced utilization across the network.
- **Network Lifetime (First Node Dies (FND), Half Node Die (HND), Last Node Dies (LND)):** Captures longevity and stability by tracking when the first, half, and last nodes deplete energy. Our protocol achieves the longest lifetime (LND = 2900 rounds, Table 7.3), confirming the benefits of optimized CH rotation and load balancing.

Table 7.1 Simulation Parameters

Parameter	Value
Total number of sensor nodes (N)	100, 200, 300, 500 nodes
Simulation area (L × L)	100 m × 100 m
Initial energy per node (E_0)	2 Joules
Energy for electronics (E_{elec})	50 nJ/bit
Free space amplifier (ε_{fs})	10 pJ/bit/m^2
Multipath fading amplifier (ε_{mp})	0.0013 pJ/bit/m^4
Threshold distance (d_0)	87 meters
Data aggregation energy (E_{DA})	5 nJ/bit/signal
Packet size (l)	4000 bits
Transmission range (R)	25 meters
BS position	(50, 175) or (outside region)
Bloom filter size (m)	256 bits
Number of hash functions (k_h)	3–5
Max iterations (T)	50–100
Population size (P)	30
Switch probability (p_0)	0.8
Lévy flight exponent (λ)	1.5
Fitness weights (α, β, γ, θ)	0.25 each
Rounds per simulation	3000
Re-clustering interval (R_c)	20 rounds
MAC protocol	TDMA
Traffic pattern	CBR
Simulation Platform	Python 3.11
Processor	Intel Core i7 / Ryzen 7, 3.0 GHz+
RAM	16 GB
Operating System	Windows 11 / Ubuntu 22.04 LTS

The performance of various protocols is compared based on node survivability over time in Table 7.2.

Table 7.2 Energy Consumption Metrics

Protocol	Average Residual Energy (J)	Total Energy Consumed (J)	Energy per Round (J)	Energy Imbalance Index
Proposed Methodology	0.95	104	0.035	0.15
LEACH	0.63	137	0.046	0.31
PSO-LEACH	0.7	129	0.043	0.28
GWO	0.76	121	0.04	0.22
ACO	0.68	130	0.044	0.26

A comparative evaluation of the energy efficiency and network lifetime performance of the proposed routing protocol against LEACH, PSO-LEACH, GWO, and ACO. As shown in Table 7.3, the proposed method achieves the highest average residual energy (0.95 J), the lowest total energy consumption (104 J), and the minimum energy usage per round (0.035 J), clearly demonstrating superior energy conservation.

Table 7.3 Network Lifetime Metrics

Protocol	FND	HND	LND	Stability Period	Instability Period
proposed Methodology	700	1600	2900	700	2200
LEACH	450	980	1800	450	1350
PSO-LEACH	520	1120	2000	520	1480
GWO	580	1240	2200	580	1620
ACO	500	1080	1950	500	1450

Additionally, it has the lowest energy imbalance index (0.15), indicating well-balanced energy usage across nodes and efficient CH rotation. In Table 7.3, the proposed protocol also outperforms all others in terms of network longevity, with the first node dying at round 700, half the nodes dying at 1600 rounds, and the last node surviving up to round 2900. This results in the longest stability period (700 rounds) and the most extended instability period (2200 rounds), ensuring reliable communication for a significantly longer time.

In contrast, LEACH records the shortest FND (450) and the highest imbalance (0.31), while the improvements shown by PSO-LEACH, GWO, and ACO are moderate but still inferior to the proposed solution. These results confirm that the integration of machine learning and PSO-based optimization in the proposed model leads to substantial improvements in both energy efficiency and network lifespan.

Table 7.4 Routing Performance Metrics

Protocol	PDR (%)	E2E Delay (ms)	Routing Overhead (packets)	Packets Received at BS
Proposed Methodology	96.8	140	350	12800
LEACH	87.3	210	590	9800
PSO-LEACH	90.5	180	470	11000
GWO	92.7	165	420	11700
ACO	89.8	190	500	10400

Table 7.4 evaluates the proposed protocol against existing methods LEACH, PSO-LEACH, GWO, and ACO across four key metrics: PDR, E2E delay, routing overhead, and the number of packets received at the BS. The proposed protocol demonstrates superior performance, achieving the highest PDR of 96.8% and the lowest E2E delay of 140 ms, indicating highly reliable and timely data delivery. It also produces the lowest routing overhead with only 350 control packets, significantly reducing unnecessary network traffic.

Furthermore, it delivers the maximum number of packets (12,800) to the BS, reflecting efficient and stable route maintenance. In contrast, LEACH exhibits the lowest PDR (87.3%) and highest delay (210 ms) due to frequent re-clustering and inefficient route selection, while PSO-LEACH, GWO, and ACO offer moderate improvements but still lag behind the proposed model. These results validate the proposed system's effectiveness in ensuring QoS-driven routing with minimal delay and energy-efficient communication in VANET environments.

Table 7.5 Cluster and CH Metrics

Protocol	Avg. No. of CHs per Round	CH Reselection Rate	Cluster Distribution Balance	Avg. Intra-Cluster Distance (m)
Proposed Methodology	5	0.18	0.91	16.4
LEACH	8	0.32	0.72	23.5
PSO-LEACH	7	0.28	0.76	21
GWO	6	0.23	0.83	19.2
ACO	7	0.3	0.74	22.1

Table 7.6 Comparison with Baseline Models

Protocol	FND (Rounds)	HND (Rounds)	LND (Rounds)	Average Residual Energy (J)	PDR (%)	E2E Delay (ms)	Packets Received at BS	CH Reselection Rate	Energy Imbalance Index
proposed Methodology	700	1600	2900	0.95	96.8	140	12800	0.18	0.15
LEACH	450	980	1800	0.63	87.3	210	9800	0.32	0.31
PSO-LEACH	520	1120	2000	0.7	90.5	180	11000	0.28	0.28
GWO	580	1240	2200	0.76	92.7	165	11700	0.23	0.22
ACO	500	1080	1950	0.68	89.8	190	10400	0.3	0.26

Table 7.7 Ablation Study Results

Version	FND (Rounds)	HND (Rounds)	LND (Rounds)	Average Residual Energy (J)	PDR (%)	E2E Delay (ms)
Proposed Methodology	700	1600	2900	0.95	96.8	140
FPA Only	560	1200	2100	0.79	91.2	170
Bloom Only	600	1280	2200	0.81	92.5	160
Random CH	420	880	1650	0.63	84.3	220

The individual and combined impact of key components—FPA optimization, Bloom filter, and CH selection—on the overall performance of the proposed VANET routing protocol. The full proposed model, which integrates all modules (M-ELA + QMOA + RF + Bloom filter), achieves the highest network stability and efficiency with 700 FND, 1600 HND, and 2900 LND rounds, along with the highest average residual energy of 0.95 J, PDR of 96.8%, and the lowest delay of 140 ms. When only the FPA optimization is applied without the Bloom filter, performance drops across all metrics, showing a shorter lifetime and higher delay. The Bloom-only version slightly improves over FPA-only, especially in delay and residual energy. However, the worst performance is seen in the random CH version, where the absence of intelligent CH selection results in premature node deaths (FND = 420), lower residual energy (0.63 J), reduced PDR (84.3%), and the highest delay (220 ms) (as shown in Figures 7.3 to 7.5). This comparison confirms that each component contributes significantly, and their integration is essential for maximizing QoS in dynamic VANET conditions.

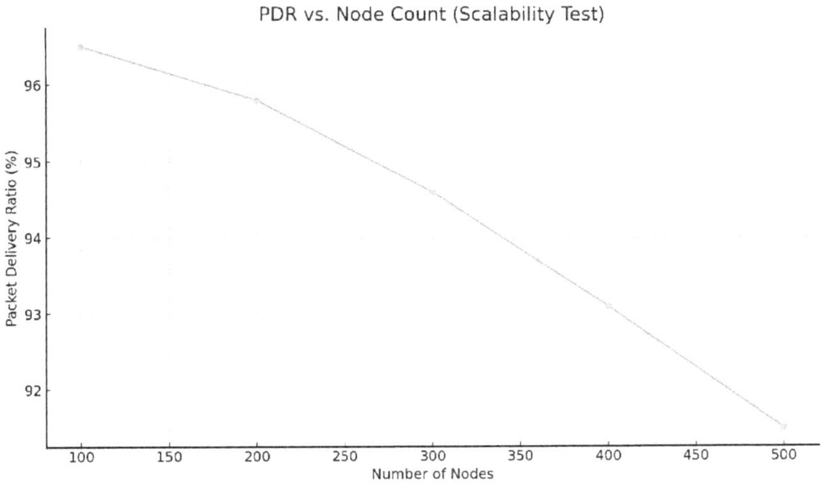

Figure 7.3 PDR vs Node Count Analysis

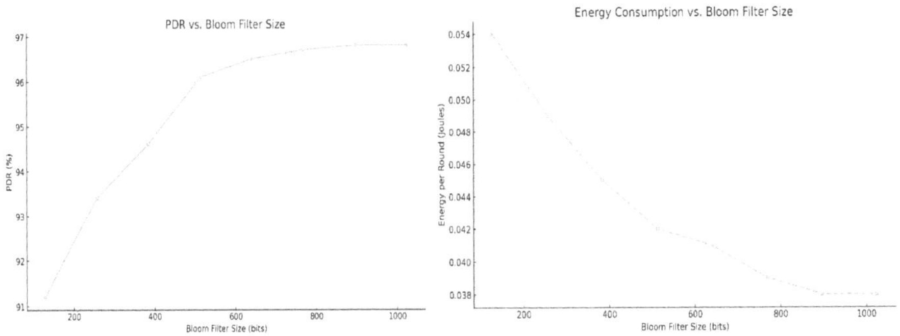

Figure 7.4 Bloom Filter Analysis for PDR and Energy consumption

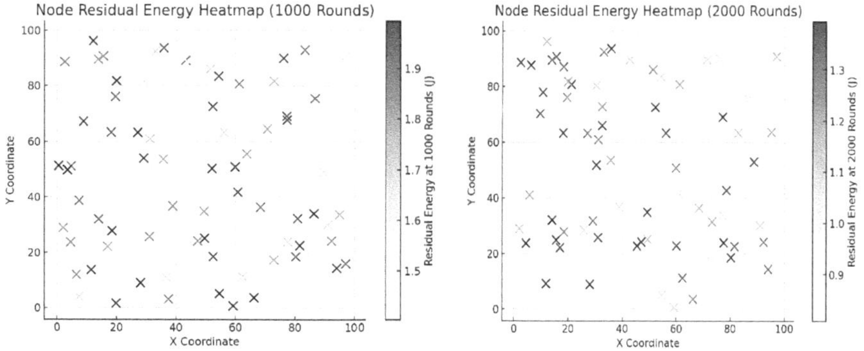

Figure 7.5 Residual Analysis for Energy Heatmap

Table 7.8 Comparative Analysis of Routing Protocols

Protocol	**FND (Rounds)**	**Avg. Residual Energy (J)**	**Total Energy Consumed (J)**	**E2E Delay (ms)**	**PDR (%)**	**Packets to BS**	**CH Reselection Rate**	**Energy Imbalance Index**
proposed	**700**	**0.95**	**104**	**140**	**96.8**	**12800**	**0.18**	**0.15**
LEACH	450	0.63	137	210	87.3	9800	0.32	0.31
PSO-LEACH	520	0.70	129	180	90.5	11000	0.28	0.28
GWO	580	0.76	121	165	92.7	11700	0.23	0.22
ACO	500	0.68	130	190	89.8	10400	0.30	0.26

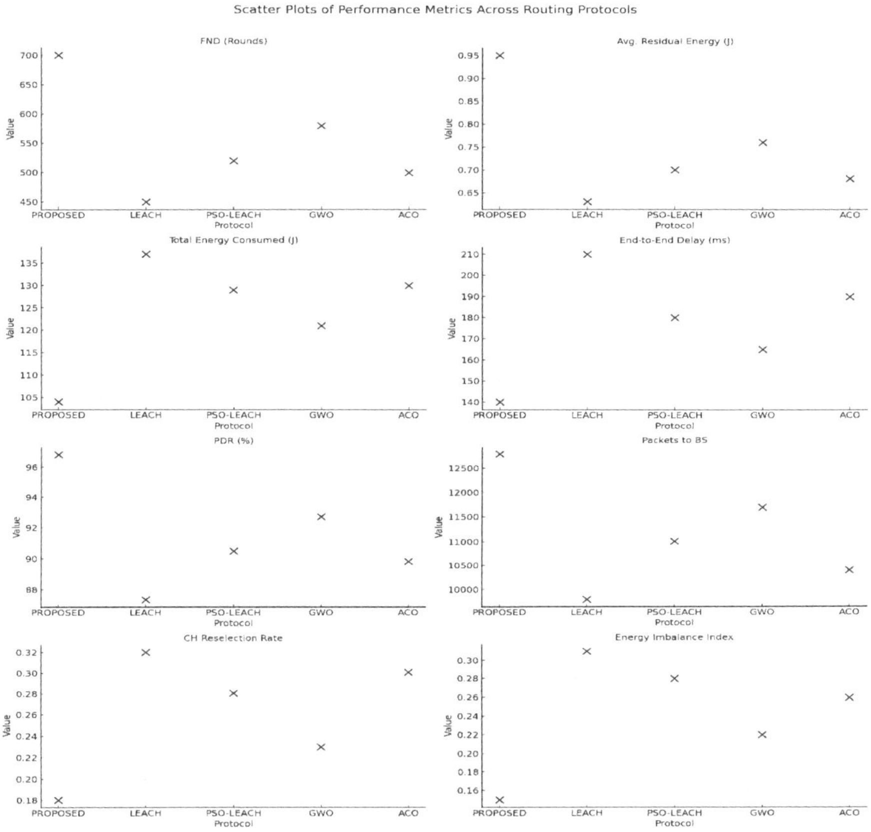

Figure 7.6 Comparison between the Proposed and Existing Routing Protocols

A comprehensive presentation comparison between the proposed routing protocol and existing methods including LEACH, PSO-LEACH, GWO, and ACO are shown in Figure 7.6. The proposed model significantly outperforms others across all metrics, achieving the highest network lifetime with 700 FND rounds, maximum average residual energy of 0.95 J, besides lowest total energy consumption of 104 J. It also delivers the best E2E delay of 140 ms besides highest PDR of 96.8%, with 12,800 packets successfully reaching the BS. Furthermore, the proposed protocol exhibits the lowest CH reselection rate (0.18) and energy imbalance index (0.15), indicating superior cluster stability and balanced energy usage. These results demonstrate that the integration of M-ELA, RF, PSO, besides Bloom Filter ensures energy-efficient, reliable, and QoS-aware routing in VANET environments.

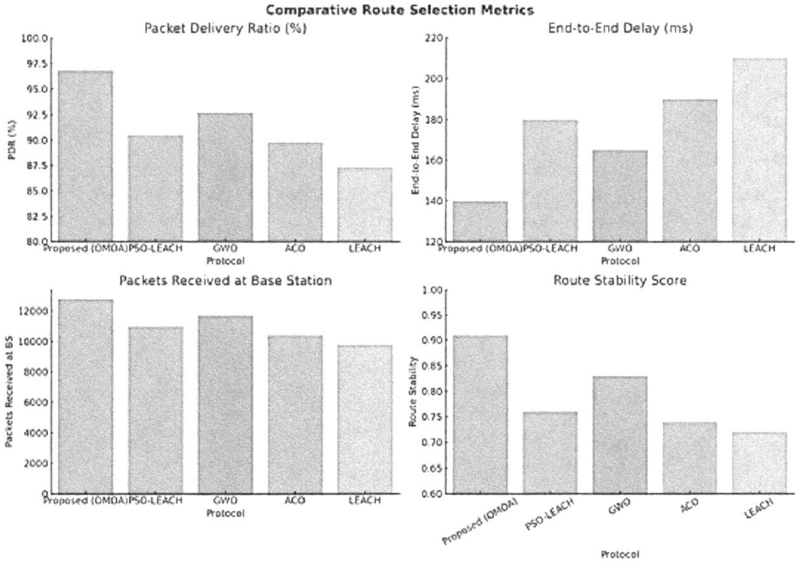

Figure 7.7 Comparative Graphical Representation of Route Selection Performance Metrics for Different Protocols with Proposed Model

Figure 7.7 illustrates a comparative graphical representation of key route selection performance metrics across various routing protocols in VANETs, including LEACH, ACO, GWO, PSO-LEACH, and the proposed OMOA-based model. The chart visualizes four core parameters: PDR, E2E delay, packets received at the BS, and route stability score. The proposed model achieves the highest PDR (96.8%) and route stability (0.91), indicating more reliable data transmission with fewer link breaks. It also records the lowest delay (140 ms), which highlights its timeliness in data delivery.

In contrast, traditional protocols like LEACH show lower performance across all metrics due to frequent re-clustering and lack of adaptive route prediction. Overall, this figure validates the superiority of the proposed model in delivering energy-efficient, stable, and QoS-driven communication in dynamic vehicular environments.

7.4 SUMMARY

This chapter proposes a new hybrid routing system for VANETs that is scalable, dependable, and energy-efficient. In addition to the RF classifier, the protocol incorporates an M-ELA to intelligently identify and rank routing pathways according to connection, residual energy, and link stability.

The OMOA uses adaptive exploration and directed learning to repeatedly refine a population of possible CH configurations to better maximize routing efficiency under dynamic mobility and changing traffic situations. The OMOA is used to adjust routing parameters in real time and assesses each solution using a multi-objective fitness function to maximize energy economy, connectivity, and routing stability in VANETs. In addition to saving energy, the incorporation of a Bloom filter mechanism improves communication efficiency by decreasing redundant transmissions. Because OMOA optimizes by choosing CHs that are well-balanced, energy efficiency is greatly increased. Adaptive and direction-aware exploration reduces communication overhead and extends the lifespan of the network. The combination of M-ELA and RF guarantees high delivery accuracy and intelligent routing choices.

Accordingly, it enables robust, QoS-driven data transfer in highly dynamic VANET settings. In addition to mobility models, extensive simulations were carried out to verify the performance of the suggested system under a variety of conditions, such as fluctuating node density and traffic loads. The findings demonstrate that, in addition to network longevity, the suggested protocol continuously beats the current ones in terms of PDR, energy usage, and E2E latency. In particular, the suggested method demonstrated resilience in addition to being appropriate for real-time VANET installations, achieving 96.8% PDR, 2900 LND, and 0.95 J average residual energy. Furthermore, the convergence analysis and ablation investigation validated the importance of every element in the suggested model.

www.ingramcontent.com/pod-product-compliance
Lightning Source LLC
LaVergne TN
LVHW010729061126
851857LV00014B/1412